"How to be a Social Entrepreneur is an essential read for any aspiring or existing social entrepreneur. Full of practical examples of real life social enterprise scenarios and written in Robert's usual uncomplicated format, this book has elements everyone in this sector can implement in their aims to make a difference and harvest a social profit."

Marc Davies, Wales Co-operative Centre Limited, walescoop.com

"As a director of a community led Community Interest Company confronting both the challenges and opportunities for a social enterprise working with the Public sector I found this book wide ranging, accessible and rather reassuring. It tells me what I need to know in language I can understand."

Jenny Morris Bradshaw, Hartismere Health and Care CIC, Suffolk

"You've got to get your hands dirty if you want to be a social entrepreneur – don't pontificate just do it. Grit under the nails and hard work is what counts if you want to build a successful social enterprise, after all you're building a business not going on a Sunday stroll. This very practical book will guide you as to what it takes to be a social entrepreneur. Enjoy it and then do it!"

Lord Andrew Mawson OBE, author of *The Social Entrepreneur: Making Communities Work*, amawsonpartnerships.com

"Social enterprises need social entrepreneurs. This book will help you decide is you've got what it takes to be one."

Peter Couchman, Chief Executive, Plunkett Foundation, plunkett.co.uk

"A comprehensive, accessible and valuable guide for those setting out on the social enterprise journey and reassuring advice for those already well on the road. I was genuinely impressed by how comprehensive it is!"

Peter Holbrook, CEO, Social Enterprise Coalition, socialenterprise.org.uk

"Anybody with a passing interest in creating a better world should read this book. Robert skillfully manages to hold our interest with a variety of real-life case studies while equipping us with all the tools we need to imagine, establish and grow our own social enterprises."

Paul Fleckney, Budding Social Entrepreneur, Melbourne, Australia

"In this time of global economic recovery, we need more social enterprises to champion the architect of change to make the world a better place for all. Robert's book is a treasure filled with practical insight and knowledge that will give you the edge to start, grow a sustainable and successful social enterprise!"

Stephen Gyasi-Kwaw, CEO /Founder Youth Enhancement Int. Host Global Entrepreneurship Week -Ghana, Fellow of School for Social Entrepreneurs UK

"A refreshing take on the social enterprise phenomenon, with a welcome emphasis on the nitty gritty aspects; I particularly enjoyed the section on sales, which is a fundamental topic too often neglected."

Andy Brady, '3rd Sector Futures', Anglia Ruskin University, anglia.ac.uk

"Robert offers plenty of practical advice, illustrated by examples of people who are already out there doing their bit to change society for good. So if you want to change the world, but aren't quite sure where to start, then this is the book for you."

Rob Greenland, www.thesocialbusiness.co.uk

How to be a Social entrepreneur

MAKE MONEY

change the

& WORLD

ROBERT ASHTON

CAPSTONE

Library of Congress Cataloguing-in-Publication Data (to follow)

ISBN 9780857080608 (Print), ISBN 9780857081377 (Ebook),
ISBN 9780857080622 (ePub), ISBN 9780857081377 (eMobi)

A catalogue record for this book is available from the British Library.

Set in 10 on 13 pt Meridien by Toppan Best-set Premedia Limited

Printed in Great Britain by TJ International Ltd, Padstow, Cornwall

Contents

Acknowledgements

Writing a book is perhaps as close (being a man) as I can ever get to having a baby. You court a number of commissioning editors before finally clinching a deal. Then the project grows inside you until eventually you go into a literary labour and force it out. Next it screams out for attention on Amazon and from bookstores around the world, demanding attention and, we all hope, winning the admiration of many. And of course you also have the launch party to wet its head.

This is my 12th book and so to develop the analogy, you'd think it would pop out in a flash with little pain. If only that were the case! A book on social enterprise needs a lot of careful pre-natal research. This particular baby has emerged into a world where many people have strong views on social enterprise and not everybody agrees. I'd like to thank those I've consulted for their generous input. Not all are mentioned and some were ignored, but that's life I guess!

So who else deserves thanks for their part in making this book possible? Well we have to start with Ellen Hallsworth who saw the potential and a deal was struck over coffee at the Tate Modern. Her assistant, Jenny Ng, ran an expert, gently critical eye over the manuscript, helping me knock off the rough edges and fill in a few gaps. And of course the marketing team has also played a key role in this book arriving in your hand.

My labour pains were eased by my team here at Turnpike Farm. Bella kept our other work commitments at bay whilst Jess checked the first draft and made sure the case studies were accurate.

Finally of course, it fell upon Belinda my long suffering wife to hold my hand, offer soothing words and stroke my anxious brow as I pushed all 50 000 words out. Without her tolerance, fortitude and common sense I would surely have died in labour.

Introduction

My good friend Edward, an IT expert, mentioned that I was writing this book to one of his clients. They are long established advisers working in the charity sector who also run training workshops for people wanting to start social enterprises. Their response illustrates perfectly why this book has such an important job to do.

'Who wants to read a book about how to be a social entrepreneur?' they said, seemingly surprised that anyone would do such a thing. And that is the problem this book seeks to address. The fact is that for those who want to make a difference, and do it in a way that is financially sustainable; this book is an essential read. It tells you how to do change the world and make money, by becoming a social entrepreneur.

Traditionally the weak and vulnerable in society have been helped along by charitable giving. Coffee mornings, gala dinners and sponsored sporting endeavours and street collections, together with public funding have enabled the charity sector to grow to meet the ever present need.

As funding tightened, so social enterprise became fashionable, but it was never really taken as seriously as it ought. Some of course rose to the challenge magnificently, transforming lives, taking control and leading the way. Others saw it as a route to more funding and never really believed any social enterprise could be self sustaining.

The second decade of the 21st century marked a significant shift in the way people see the world. For the duration of this decade, it is unlikely that politicians in any nation will have money to spare. Funding for health, education, social welfare and more will be bitterly fought over and barely sufficient when won.

Climate change has leapt from a fringe anxiety to a major driver of behavioural change, by everyone and almost every organisation around the world. Change creates opportunity as well as confusion and a new generation of community organisations is emerging to generate power, grow local food and re-build communities.

As the pundits are increasingly predicting, tomorrow's entrepreneur will be a social entrepreneur. More confident shaking hands than shaking a collecting tin; more confident negotiating innovative, collaborative partnerships with those able to help them further the cause and more confident that profit is good, because of the freedom it gives you to do good.

If you want to take control of your future, perhaps of your organisation's future too, you need to become a social entrepreneur. Making money alone is no longer enough. You have to visibly, measurably and enthusiastically make a difference too!

Part One
What

1

The Essence of Social Entrepreneurship

'The worst sin toward our fellow creatures is not to hate them, but to be indifferent to them: that's the essence of inhumanity.'

George Bernard Shaw – *The Devil's Disciple*, Act 2

A new way to view the world

Social entrepreneurs are people who see the world differently. They see opportunity where others see challenge. They see potential where others see problems. What makes them different from other entrepreneurs is that they have a very strong social conscience. Creating vast personal wealth or a large corporation does not excite them half as much as creating sustainable social change.

There is a difference clearly between a social entrepreneur and a social enterprise. This was explained to me very clearly one day by Charlotte Young who chairs the School for Social Entrepreneurs. It's obvious when you think of it. Of course one is an individual and the other an organisation but here's the point Charlotte made that most people miss:

> 'Not all social enterprises are started by social entrepreneurs and not all social entrepreneurs start social enterprises.'

The School for Social Entrepreneurs website defines a social entrepreneur as:

> 'someone who works in an entrepreneurial manner, but for public or social benefit, rather than simply to make money. Social entrepreneurs may work in ethical businesses, governmental or public bodies, quangos, or the voluntary and community sector.'

What makes a social entrepreneur?

A social entrepreneur is usually someone with a real, urgent driving passion to change something they feel strongly about. Often they have witnessed first hand the indignity of a particular social problem and decide to do something about it.

Qualified by personal experience, they are driven by a desire to right a social injustice or simply to make the world a better place. What they may lack in enterprise skills they make up for with doggedness and relentless energy. Give them the skills and you can see world-changing results.

It's really important for you to understand this difference between the social entrepreneur and a social enterprise. Some people find themselves running social enterprises by default, rather than choice. They may not have the attitude, skills or experience or even desire to be a social entrepreneur. More often than not it is an additional responsibility that's been thrust upon them by someone further up the line in their organisation.

For example:

- A Board of Trustees decide that they want the charity they govern to reduce its reliance on grants and generate income. A very capable, caring senior manager finds themselves leading in a new area they barely understand;
- A major funding source is lost and faced with imminent closure, a charity team decides to sell their services to paying clients to subsidise service delivery. In theory, this is possible. In practice it means learning to sell and market to a discerning customer group what has until then only been offered for free to the disadvantaged;
- A public sector department finds itself at risk of closure. Some jobs will transfer to a larger contractor, but most will go. The team decides to form a social enterprise and bid for the contract themselves. They also plan to win work from neighbouring authorities to create the additional budget they need to survive. Driven by concern for their jobs and service users, they are taking a giant leap into the unknown.

Social entrepreneurs, as the School for Social Entrepreneurs suggests, can be found in all kinds of organisations, as well as working on their own. In fact as my own experience illustrates, you don't need permission to be a social entrepreneur. You just need the passion and drive to make a difference, coupled with the enterprise skills to make it happen.

Finally, here are three well known examples of social entrepreneurs who have started very successful social enterprise.

Michael Young (of Dartington) – helped set up more than 60 organisations in his lifetime, including the Open University, the Consumers' Association and the School for Social Entrepreneurs.

He became a political researcher early in his career which gave him an insight into how communities worked and were influenced. His vision for a more equal society grew out of this work. Empowering individuals to take greater responsibility for themselves and their neighbourhoods became a theme that ran though his work.

Jamie Oliver set up Fifteen to provide opportunities for disadvantaged young people to enter the catering industry. His own background, raised in an Essex pub and leaving school without qualifications to attend catering college, was far from unique. His big break came in 1999 when spotted by the BBC whilst working at The River Café in Fulham. His media career grew from there.

As well as founding Fifteen, Oliver has campaigned widely on issues close to his heart. He bought the varying quality of school dinners to national attention, doing much to improve what schools offer young people to eat.

Muhammad Yunus was a university academic who set up the micro-finance organisation Grameen Bank in

Bangladesh. It was witnessing a famine in 1974 that prompted him to explore ways of increasing the self sufficiency of the rural poor.

He recognised that very small loans, although they could make a huge difference, were not being made because the poor could offer no security to the bank. His Grameen Bank developed a business model where the whole community took responsibility for borrowers repaying their loans.

Leadership beyond authority

You do not need authority to lead social change. Too often it is those in authority who are holding back the change you want to see. Of course there is a fine line between rebellion and campaigning for positive change. Perhaps the difference is in the extent to which others have a hunger to see you succeed. For example:

→ Without the Suffragettes' very public protests in the early 20th century it might have been many more years before British women won the right to vote.

→ Without Nelson Mandela and his fellow ANC campaigners, it would be harder for black people in South Africa to start and grow their own businesses.

→ Without Stephen Whittle, a campaigning academic and founder of the organisation 'Press for Change', transgender people in the UK would probably be facing greater prejudice.

You could say that these three were all political campaigners. In part you would be right, but what drove them was their desire for social change. Challenging the political status quo was just one way they brought about the changes they wanted to see, for those they cared deeply about. Each of the examples above fits with the School for Social Entrepreneurs's definition of a social entrepreneur.

But what, you might ask, about some of the other campaigns we have seen in recent years? Are all of them examples of social entrepreneurship? Take 'Real Fathers for Justice' as an example. It's a lobby group campaigning for a better deal for divorced dads. Like the Suffragettes, their members chain themselves to railings and get arrested. Like Nelson Mandela, their members are prepared to go to prison for their beliefs. The difference perhaps is that they are campaigning for their own rights, rather than for the wider social or public good.

What works

To bring about the social and environmental change they want to see, social entrepreneurs often bump into political barriers. What works for them is that they want to change the lives of others more than they want to change their own life. Use this as an Acid Test of any social entrepreneur you meet.

Leading Beyond Authority is the ethos that underpins the work of the independent and international leadership development charity, Common Purpose. The organisation runs leadership development courses in 13 countries around the world. The courses bring together people from the private, public and not-for-profit sectors.

The organisation takes people from a broad cross section of the community and exposes them through a learning experience to the complex issues and leadership challenges in various sectors, cities, regions and countries. The courses have a local, city, regional, national or international focus.

The charity's founder, Julia Middleton, set up Common Purpose because she realised how few people have the opportunity to really understand how to lead in partnership and work collaboratively with a clear understanding of context and how decisions impact society, organisations and individuals. 'We all know the sector we work in', she told me, 'but increasingly those sectors are independent. How can you lead lasting change without an understanding of how everything fits together?'

In an age of career specialism, it is increasingly difficult for leaders to understand the impact of change in one sector upon others. Yet people's lives are in reality complex, all affected to some extent by health, education, faith, justice and commerce. To lead beyond authority effectively, it helps to be able to assemble that human jigsaw.

Moved to make a difference

For many people, programmes such as Common Purpose are the catalysts that spark their personal revolution. You might be a Common Purpose graduate, or more likely to have simply been prompted by some event to realise that you have the ability to make a real difference in perhaps a very modest way.

But a catalyst alone does not start a reaction. You'll remember from your chemistry lessons at school that you also need two or more other compounds. These, with the catalyst's help, are changed into something new.

So what are those compounds that lie within your reach, as they do with every potential social entrepreneur, waiting to be unlocked in some way? Usually they are experiential. Something that has happened in a person's life that when conditions are right, emerge to provide emotional fuel for the campaign that they choose to mount.

Remember that definition of a social entrepreneur. It is someone who works in an entrepreneurial manner for public or social benefit. Can you now recognise how some of the people you know are actually, in perhaps very modest ways, social entrepreneurs?

They are the people who actually challenge the status quo and step forward. They become sufficiently moved by what they experience or witness that they decide to do something about it. In today's world, the only way to bring about sustainable change is through being enterprising and entrepreneurial. But almost inevitably, something or a combination of different things has provoked them into action.

In the next chapter, we will look at these precursors to social entrepreneurship more closely. If you are to really succeed as a social entrepreneur, you need to dig back into your life to find the events and experiences that will combine to create what makes you uniquely placed and ably qualified for that role.

Here's my summary of this very important point:

> *Your success as a social entrepreneur will be directly proportional to the passion you feel for what you are trying to achieve. The more pain you have suffered or seen, the more passionately you will pursue your goal and the greater the impact you will have.*

Earth, wind and fire – the green dimension

With the exception of a handful of meteorites, there is nothing on this planet that was not there when it was formed. Every atom of every element that makes up our world has always been here. The catalyst that has enabled things to change, evolve and develop is sunlight. The light and warmth of the sun is all that has been added and for the foreseeable future, all that ever will.

In other words, the planet is a finite resource we all need to take great care of. The scientist James Lovelock studied the way that everything is interconnected. His Gaia theory is widely followed. It suggests that climate, atmospheric composition and sea salinity are all regulated by the world's biomass. In other words, that living things adapt in ways that enable them to best use and maintain the very finely balanced physical environment needed to support life.

Here are some issues that might motivate you to be a social entrepreneur:

➡ **Climate change** is going to change everyone's world, sometimes in very dramatic ways, as rising sea levels engulf low lying regions. Do you want to change behaviours in ways that reduce carbon emissions? New industries, such as wind generation, are emerging to provide clean electricity. Can you introduce new ways of balancing human need with our environmental impact?

➡ **Sanitation** is a global concern, from European nations pouring raw sewage into the sea to millions of people across Asia and Africa with no access to toilet facilities whatsoever. Just as the bottled water industry has done much to fund well sinking in the developing world, so too could businesses connected with the bathroom fund better sanitation with the huge health improvements this can deliver. Could this be your opportunity?

➡ **Poverty** is visible on the streets of every city in the world. Just as *The Big Issue* is slowly spreading its business model around the world, so too could you be combating poverty in a real and sustainable way. In London, there is a catering company that employs the homeless as waiters. This not only pays them a wage, but it enables them to mix with people from all walks of live without the embarrassment of being on the street. Does your career background equip you to do something similar?

➡ **Ageism** is a growing problem in Western society. Older people are going to have to remain at work for longer as few have adequate pension provision. Just as B&Q makes a point of hiring older people to provide DIY advice to shoppers, you might also have a business idea capable of employing older people in an innovative and interesting way.

The problem is that mankind is now so populous and advanced that our activities are disturbing the natural equilibrium Lovelock describes. Issues such as deforestation, intensive agriculture, pollution and the burning of fossil fuels are all changing the world faster than it can naturally adapt.

The environment is the final dimension to the social entrepreneur's world. Sustainability is only achieved when you successfully balance people, planet and profit. Neglect one and you jeopardise the others. Many would say that failure to maintain this balance is one of the reasons our world is facing environmental challenges such as climate change.

This balance between people, planet and profit is called the 'triple bottom line'.

The triple bottom line is increasingly becoming a concern for organisations of all kinds, not just those with a strong social or environmental purpose. It is of particular concern to multinationals who need to know that their local businesses and suppliers are behaving responsibly. This is because their customers and end users want to know that they are not damaging the planet, or abusing people in the pursuit of profit.

The Corporate Responsibility Coalition commissioned The London School of Economics to review what was happening in this area. Their report, titled 'The reality of rights', was published in May 2009. It concluded that; 'the activities of transnational enterprises can promote economic development and generate wealth and prosperity, thereby enhancing the realisation of a broad range of economic and social rights. On the other hand, there is no doubt that they can and do perpetrate human rights abuses affecting both workers and communities in many of the host countries in which they operate around the world'.

In the developing world at least, human rights and environmental damage seem almost always to be interlinked. The report cites a few examples:

→ Significant disruption to communities living along oil pipelines in Georgia.
→ Establishing a bauxite smelting within a protected forest in India, considered sacred by locals.
→ Acid rain from oil well gas flares in Nigeria corroding local housing.

Each of these examples, cited in the report, involve multinational corporations that in these situations at least, appear to have put profit before planet or local people.

For many, it is witnessing situations like this that prompt them to become social entrepreneurs or campaigners. Often it takes local people to see the opportunity to benefit from what might at first appear an intrusive disadvantage. Even if all they achieve is community compensation to fund projects that improve health, education, sanitation or economic survival.

Green Light Trust

In 1988, Ric Edelmann and Nigel Hughes travelled to Papua New Guinea in search of primary rainforest. It had been their long-held wish to witness this most prolific and spectacular ecosystem.

With local tribesmen, they trekked through the dense Hunstein forest of the Upper Sepik, home to some of the 34 different birds of paradise, and many species of flora and fauna then still unclassified.

They learnt that the entire region – 2,000 square miles of pristine forest – was earmarked for the biggest logging operation yet to hit Papua New Guinea. There and then they pledged to support the people in protecting their unique homeland.

They were also asked what was happening in the UK to protect our woodlands and wild spaces for future generations.

Ric and Nigel's commitment to developing these initiatives led to the forming of Green Light Trust. Ric, Nigel and their team have helped many British communities establish, maintain and enjoy their own community woodland. The process helps people reconnect with their environment, get to know their neighbours and most importantly of all, create wild-spaces to be enjoyed by future generations.

The charity also provides environmental training for schools and business as well as working with communities.

There really is no escaping the fact that people, planet and profit are all equally important to the social entrepreneur.

In summary

- Not all social enterprises are started by social entrepreneurs and not all social entrepreneurs start social enterprises.
- Social entrepreneurs can be found in all walks of life and sometimes in the most unlikely jobs.
- Passion and sometimes pain are what drive most social entrepreneurs.
- What you do is often dictated by experiencing or witnessing injustice.
- You don't need to wait for permission to be entrepreneurial: just do it!
- People, planet and profit are all equally important to us all.

Find out more

School for Social Entrepreneurs	sse.org.uk
Fifteen	fifteen.net
Grameen Bank	grameen-info.org
Press for Change	pfc.org.uk
Real Fathers for Justice	realfathersforjustice.org
Common Purpose	commonpurpose.org.uk
The Corporate Responsibility Coalition	corporate-responsibility.org
Green Light Trust	greenlighttrust.org

2

Social Enterprise – Past, Present and Future

'When the first baby laughed for the first time, the laugh broke into a thousand pieces and they all went skipping about, and that was the beginnings of fairies.'

J M Barrie – *Peter Pan*, Act 1

In the beginning

Social enterprise is no fairy tale. Social entrepreneurs have always existed and always will. There have been businesses we would recognise as social enterprises for as long as there have been businesses.

What has changed is the language of social enterprise. Let's start with a definition. The Social Enterprise Coalition is a national organisation that represents and supports social enterprise in the UK. Their definition is this:

> 'Social enterprises are businesses trading for social and environmental purposes.'

This is perhaps the best of the many definitions you will encounter. It makes it clear that a social enterprise is a business first and foremost. What sets these businesses apart from others is that they are trading for social or environmental purposes. In other words they set out to make a difference as well as a profit. More usually than not, much of the profit they make is reinvested in their cause.

Arguably, until the Industrial Revolution, all businesses traded for social and environmental purposes. That is because:

→ Businesses were small and local – their customers, employees and owners all formed the same community. It made sense to be popular.
→ Businesses relied upon local resources to provide most of the raw materials they required. They instinctively worked in ways that sustained those resources.
→ Britain was sparsely populated and transport poor. Communities recognised the interdependence of their local economy and worked together to protect it.

Of course life and enterprise were not perfect in those days. People did not know the full repercussions of all that they did. There was little education and people mostly learned by word of mouth and experience. They did what they knew would work.

With the Industrial Revolution came dramatic change. Mechanisation created opportunities for mass production. People migrated from the countryside to work in the newly built urban mills and factories. The towns grew to accommodate the influx of workers. People became distanced from their roots and work became something you did in a factory, rather than simply being a way of life.

Some of the early industrialists exploited their workers, their suppliers and the environment. They focused solely on the immediate opportunity to make large profits. Many grew very wealthy and went on to become philanthropists.

Andrew Carnegie emigrated from Scotland to the USA with his parents as a child. He worked his way up from factory worker to one of America's most successful industrialists.

He gave away most of his wealth before he died, establishing schools, libraries and universities across the USA. He also funded a pension scheme for his employees.

His philosophy for life was simple:

- Learn all you can in the first third.
- Earn all you can in the second third.
- Give it all away in the final third.

Quakers

Some of the best known early social entrepreneurs were Quakers. The movement started in the 1640s and has always been known for its strong focus on social activism. Quakers believe we are all equal and all deserve an equal chance. They were strong campaigners against slavery.

Their values drove Quaker entrepreneurs to run their businesses in a way that made life better for those who worked for them. Their strong social purpose meant that the businesses they ran would clearly meet today's definition of a social enterprise. For example:

→ **The Gurney family** were large landowners in Norfolk and founders of Barclays Bank. People who worked on their country estate were provided with good housing and fair pay. My grandmother was born on their estate, attended the school they supported and worked for them as a Housemaid.
→ **The Cadbury family** – John Cadbury started making drinking chocolate in 1831. The business grew to become a major employer in Birmingham. The family created the village of Bournville to house, educate and meet the health needs of their workforce. The family Trust remains to this day a major grant maker, promoting social justice.

Many Quaker businesses today retain the strong social values of the movement.

Jane Lambert (www.nipclaw.com) is a Barrister specialising in intellectual property, media, entertainment and competition law. She is a Quaker and says; 'small businesses need legal protection for their intellectual assets at least as much as big business. My practice gives them the services they need at a price they can afford.'

Cooperatives

In 1761 a group of Scottish weavers at Fenwick in Ayrshire started buying oatmeal collectively. They bought it in large sacks and sold the contents on to their members at a lower price than the local shops. This Fenwick Weavers' Society is considered by many to be the first cooperative.

The Rochdale Society of Equitable Pioneers was established in 1844. Its founders wrote the 'Rochdale Principles', on which the modern cooperative movement is based.

Others followed and the movement grew. By the late 19th century, there were many cooperative retail societies. These operated shops that sold goods at prices high enough to maintain profitability but low enough to be affordable by their members. Profits were distributed to members as dividends.

Cooperatives are jointly owned and democratically controlled by their members. The members are the beneficiaries of the business. Cooperatives are amongst the earliest examples of social enterprises.

Cooperatives UK defines a cooperative as: 'An autonomous association of persons united voluntarily to meet their common economic, social, and cultural needs and aspirations through a jointly-owned and democratically-controlled enterprise'.

The founders' 'Rochdale principles'	Today's cooperative principles
1. Open membership	1. Voluntary and open membership
2. Democratic control	2. Democratic member control
3. Dividend on purchase	3. Member economic participation
4. Limited interest on capital	4. Autonomy and independence
5. Political and religious neutrality	5. Education, training and information
6. Cash trading	6. Cooperation between cooperatives
7. Promotion of education	7. Concern for community

At the moment

Over the past few years, the social enterprise movement has grown substantially. This growth has come from:

→ Entrepreneurs setting up businesses where the social purpose is paramount;
→ People wanting to start businesses that do more than simply make money;
→ Charities setting up trading subsidiaries to generate income.

All have recognised that the best way to bring about the changes they want to see is to take control and do it themselves.

The Big Issue

Entrepreneur Gordon Roddick, husband of the late Anita Roddick of Body Shop fame, set up *The Big Issue* with John Bird in 1991. John Bird was raised in an orphanage and slept rough in London for many years. He also served several prison sentences.

John Bird realised that soup kitchens and hand-outs were not helping homeless people escape life on the streets. He had worked in the print industry and had seen a street newspaper in New York called *Street News*. He persuaded Gordon Roddick to invest in the business that enabled homeless people to earn money by selling copies of *The Big Issue* on the streets.

Copies of *The Big Issue* can now be purchased on almost every High Street in Britain. The business has sales of more than £3.5m each year and has helped thousands of homeless people regain their confidence and self respect and return to mainstream life.

Wayland Radio

At the age of 52, Dave Hatherly left his job working for BBC East Midlands and moved to Norfolk. He no longer needed to work full time but certainly did not want to retire. Aware of the way local radio stations could inform, connect and strengthen communities he decided to set up Wayland Community Radio. Starting a business just to make money held little appeal.

His research showed that many people in his area lived alone, with few neighbours and poor public transport. There were also large populations of migrant workers, all living a long way from their home. He brought together a team and successfully bid for funding to get the radio station licensed and on air.

Wayland Radio is now up and running, broadcasting in English and Polish to an increasing audience of listeners. They also have a growing roster of talented, volunteer presenters and provide communication skills training to businesses, youth groups and charities. The station is also attracting advertisers, makes money and clearly makes a difference.

Social enterprise may be a modern phrase, but the concept has always been with us. As these two examples show, it also makes sense in today's complex world. Social enterprise allows organisations and individuals to bring about the changes they want to see.

In the future

The 21st century has already delivered seismic change to our society. Many of the things we came to accept as normal in the last century, have been overturned. It was after all only after the Second World War that people became accustomed to a time of plenty. Concerns about climate change, communities where worklessness and benefits dependence are considered the norm, and fast rising energy costs are forcing change and challenging what we all take for granted.

In 2009, David Cameron, before he became Prime Minister talked in a speech about a 'radical redistribution of power from the State to citizens'. He went on to describe this shift as a move from 'bureaucracy to democracy.' His Government, elected in 2010, placed more emphasis on individuals and communities to decide what they want for themselves, then create it. This has set the scene for the continued growth in social enterprise since then.

It is also true to say that social enterprises weather the storm of recession better than other businesses. A 'survey' conducted by the Social Enterprise Coalition in 2009 revealed that despite the UK being in recession:

➡ 56% saw turnover increase (2007/8) against only 28% of businesses in general;

➡ 48% were expecting to grow against just 24% of small businesses in general.

So why do social enterprises do so much better in a downturn that businesses established purely to make money? I think it's because we are all becoming much more aware of business ethics and values. When all else is equal, we increasingly choose to spend our money with enterprises that:

➡ Invest in people rather than exploit them;
➡ Protect the environment rather than destroy it;
➡ Invest in society's vulnerable people, rather than amass huge wealth.

The Fair Trade Foundation was set up in 1992. It was established to develop and promote trading structures and practices that favour, rather than exploit the poor and disadvantaged.

The organisation achieves this by encouraging and assessing organisations against the Fair Trade standard and licensing those that qualify to use the Fair Trade logo. It also promotes Fair Trade widely and vitally, raises public awareness of Fair Trade to generate consumer demand for Fair Trade products.

UK sales of Fair Trade products are growing fast, more than doubling between 2005 and 2009. Many large corporations such as Starbucks and Nestle now sell Fair Trade products. This shows that growing consumer demand for Fair Trade is encouraging even the largest organisations to demonstrate their commitment to those who grow and process their ingredients.

Many predict that the social enterprise movement has reached its tipping point and is poised to grow at a similarly dramatic rate over the next few years.

It used to be simple. The bank lent you money, the supermarket sold you food, the council emptied your waste bin and the charity helped those facing disadvantage. Today things are less straightforward. For example:

- Banks give customers legal advice helplines and car breakdown cover;[1]
- Supermarkets lend money and receive public funding to employ disadvantaged people;
- Councils own hotels, sell business services[2] and invest money they've collected speculatively in overseas banks;
- Charities such as Oxfam are now major High Street retailers.

Over the past few years we have seen many of the boundaries that separate public, private and voluntary sector become blurred. Social enterprises can emerge from each of these sectors. They can also create new kinds of enterprise that simply don't fit with, or actually combine the existing models. This can appear both exciting and daunting. We all enjoy the novelty of the new and welcome the familiarity of the established.

Social entrepreneurs, that is people like you and me, recognise and seize the opportunities these changes create. We take advantage of what puzzles others about the enterprise land-

---

[1] Barclays Additions Active account (www.bank.barclays.co.uk)
[2] 'Barnham Broom agreement', 1 October 2009 (www.breckland.gov.uk)

scape. We configure products, people and perceptions in new and interesting ways to meet need and liberate individual choice and freedom.

Fermanagh Voluntary Association of the Disabled is a long established voluntary organisation that provides training, advice, practical support and social opportunities to people living with disability. They generate income by hiring out their meeting rooms to other organisations. Ten years ago they struck a deal with their local Council to set up a Community Re-paint project. Unwanted paint is brought by householders to the Council's recycling centre from where it is collected by the Association. Local decorators and paint suppliers also give their surplus stock. The association in turn passes it on to charities, other voluntary groups and people living on benefits unable to afford to buy paint to decorate their homes.

This provides employment experience for the Association's service users as well as helping local organisations and their volunteers maintain and decorate their premises. Finally it avoids perfectly good paint going into land fill.

Further signs of the growth and potential for social enterprise can be seen in and around each sector. For example:

Corporate social responsibility – until recently might have been little more than a company giving money and perhaps time to a good cause. For example, a factory sponsors the local school football club. Now it can become a point of market difference. The factory promotes the fact that the more successful it becomes, the more school football teams it can sponsor.

Kettle Chips make snack foods on both sides of the Atlantic and believe that good businesses can co-exist with nature. They have built energy efficient factories, use bio-diesel in their vehicles and are researching biodegradable packaging too.

The company also gives both money and product to support community groups around their production plants and to national conservation and wildlife charities. It is an excellent example of how good CSR can enable a company to play a real and active role in ways that are linked to the products it manufactures. At Kettle they call this community engagement 'chipping in'.

Customers will increasingly choose a supplier who (if all else is equal) invest a proportion of the profits in a worthwhile cause.

Outplaced public services – public sector services have usually been funded through taxation and not placed in competition with one another. Under a programme called the 'Right to Request', teams working within the UK health service can choose to set up a social enterprise. This means they can widen their service offer to meet service user demand. They retain funding from the health service, but only linked to what they deliver. It's an initiative that improves services, reduces costs, widens service user choice and enables people to take ownership of their enterprise and their future

Government is rolling out a direct payments programme that means users of all public services have the ability to choose. They decide how the public money allocated to them should be spent.

Community ownership – at a local level, the connection between publicly owned resources and the communities that use them have been lost. You know that your local swimming baths belong to the council and that the council is representing you. You don't however feel that you are a part owner of the swimming baths.

One reason for this disconnect is that the public sector body owning the facility might represent a population of more than a million. The neighbourhood within which its users are drawn from is often far, far smaller. New, smaller and more locally accountable organisations are being set up to take over, develop and cherish local facilities. People make more use of and take better care of facilities they feel belong to themselves and their neighbours.

Gigha is a small island in the Hebrides situated off the Scottish coast. When the company owning the island went bust, residents set about raising the money to buy the place for themselves.

They set up a company limited by guarantee to manage the island, with all residents aged over 18 eligible for membership. The cash was raised through grants, loans and local subscription and a Community Land Trust created to hold the island in community ownership in perpetuity.

Over the past few years, Gigha has seen much needed new housing, new jobs and its own wind farm. The community has moved from stagnation to growth. It is an exciting place to live and work.

The UK Government elected in 2010 introduced a 'community right to buy' scheme. This gives community organisations first option to buy and take over community assets threatened with closure.

In summary

- Social enterprises are businesses trading for social and environmental purposes.
- Social enterprise is a way of reconnecting communities in ways that have long been lost, regaining local ownership, accountability and responsibility.
- Quaker industrialists were early social entrepreneurs, successful because they invested in the communities within which they made their wealth.
- The cooperative movement with its collective benefit and strong principles is a form of social enterprise that continues to grow.
- Many of today's social enterprises are started by charities wanting greater control over their income.
- An increasing number of business starters today are starting social enterprises.
- There has probably never been a better time to start a social enterprise.

Find out more

Social Enterprise Coalition	socialenterprise.org.uk
Quakers & Business	qandb.org
Cooperatives UK	cooperatives-uk.coop
Oxfam	oxfam.org.uk
Big Issue	bigissue.co.uk
Wayland Radio	waylandradio.com
David Cameron Speech 2009	guardian.co.uk/commentisfree/ 2009/may/25/david-cameron-a-new-politics

Social Enterprise Coalition Survey	socialenterprise.org.uk/ pages/state_of_social_ enterprise.html
Fair Trade Foundation	fairtrade.org.uk
Community Re-paint	communityrepaint.org.uk

Part Two
Who

Part Two

3

You As a Social Entrepreneur

'Courage is what it takes to stand up and speak, courage is also what it takes to sit down and listen.'
Sir Winston Churchill

You are unique

One of the paradoxes of humanity is that although physiologically we are all very much the same, inside we are all very different. When we look at other people, our brain highlights and magnifies the small physical differences. But when you think about it, those differences are very small. We all share common ancestors and all feel the same emotions. In many ways, we are all predictable, yet in other ways we are all totally unique.

So what makes you unique? Let's start with your parents. Your physical and to an extent your intellectual potential is defined by your mother and father. They have genetic influence over what you are. They also shape your early life and influence your ambition, self esteem and self confidence. Your teenage rebellion was also quite natural, because to become an adult, you have to claim and assert your individuality.

In the opening pages of his autobiography '*Losing my Virginity*' Richard Branson wrote about his mother: 'when I was four years old she stopped the car a few miles from our house and made me find my way home across the fields.' He describes how she constantly set him challenges because he said, 'it would teach me the importance of stamina and a sense of direction.'

Few parents would behave like that today, 50 years later. But how much of his willingness to take risks, both personal and commercial, are the product of those early experiences? Compare this with your own childhood and attitude to risk. Ask yourself, if Branson's parents had not encouraged him to explore, would he be the successful entrepreneur he is today?

It would be easy to become disheartened as you reflect on your own early years. That would be normal too. You may recall how the poet Philip Larkin blamed parents for much of what holds us all back in adult life. His argument was that however hard they try, your parents will inevitably spoil your chances.

But life is not that simple. What shapes your future is less what experiences you have but how you respond to them. If that were not the case, life would become a depressing chronology of shortening horizons. If each experience limited your potential in some way or the other, it would be possible to predict your future with some accuracy. Luckily your uniqueness is the product of much more than your parents and your past. For example:

- Famous aviator **Amy Johnson** was born to parents wealthy enough to buy her a plane. Without their help, she may well have led a more obscure life.
- Inventor of the telephone, **Alexander Graham Bell**'s father, grandfather and brother worked on elocution and speech and his mother and wife were profoundly deaf. As a scientist, this prompted his interest in speech transmission.
- **Louis Pasteur** was prompted to research into the causes of disease by the tragic deaths of three of his children from typhoid. He became one of the pioneers of microbiology.

US psychologist Judith Rich Harris, in her book '*The Nature Assumption*' challenged the extent to which people thought parents influenced their children's personality, attitudes and behaviour. She cites the example of a family moving to an area where local people speak with a different accent. Although the parents still speak the same, their children quickly adapt to speak as others do where they are. In other words, they are more influenced by those around them than by their immediate family.

Harris proposed that three distinct systems shape personality:

→ A **relationship system** allows us to distinguish family from strangers and tell individuals apart. It could be argued that this process is what gives us prejudices and preferences.

→ A **socialization system** helps us to become members of a group and absorb the group's culture. This could be interpreted as our 'hard-wired' need to belong to a tribal group.

→ A **status system** enables us to acquire self-knowledge by measuring ourselves against others. Perhaps that's why the company you keep makes such a difference to your aspirations.

Questions to ask yourself

1. Who are the people who have most influenced you in life so far?
2. Who do you most want to be like and why?
3. Who are your heroes and in what ways do you want to be more like them?

The most successful people are those who know themselves well and are comfortable with the way they are.

You have what it takes

Entrepreneurs are people who know themselves well and have the courage to take risks. Many do this by starting a business. If you're an entrepreneur you'll understand this already. Most people follow the herd; entrepreneurs don't. At home and at work most people only choose from the options that exist. They may well push themselves to climb the career ladder to heights they find uncomfortable. Few will develop the confidence to step off the ladder and strike off in a new direction.

Entrepreneurs are different. They question what they see and willingly step into the unknown. They see opportunities where others see darkness. They see how over time, old practices become less effective and innovation can make a difference. Most of all, they see within themselves the courage and confidence to take risks and try something new.

But social entrepreneurs have another characteristic. They are driven by a passion to deliver positive change to others. That drive is often founded on personal experience of injustice, inhumanity or inequality. Often the tipping point is reached when they are told something they feel strongly about cannot be done. For example:

- → **John Bird** started the 'The Big Issue' because he'd lived on the streets and knew how providing homeless people with something to sell would raise self esteem.
- → **Camila Batmanghelidjh** started 'Kids Company' to provide practical, emotional and educational support to deprived inner city youngsters. When her father became a political prisoner in Iran, she worked with disadvantaged kids to fund her place at a UK boarding school that her family could no longer afford.
- → **Andy Kent** started his own garage near Cambridge and employs mechanics with disabilities. He was prompted by being told he could not keep his job as a motor engineer when he recovered from a brain haemorrhage that affected his mobility.

Not all social entrepreneurs start their own social enterprise. Some choose to remain within their organisation, bringing about often substantial change in the face of considerable opposition. This demands as much and sometimes more courage than walking away and setting up a new organisation from scratch.

Lance Gardner, Open Doors

Lance is a social entrepreneur working within and stretching the boundaries of the NHS.

Lance qualified as a nurse and health visitor before becoming a manager within the NHS. For many years he campaigned for front line medical services to be delivered in a way that valued clinicians and patients equally. He felt strongly that vulnerable people in particular had health problems that were too often overlooked. As he succinctly summarises the problem: 'They do not care about their health because they do not know where the next meal is coming from.'

By 2007, after some time advising the Department of Health on the establishing of Foundation Trusts, he was working in North East Lincolnshire PCT as Director of Clinical Services. The NHS was seeking bids from NHS managers to set up pathfinder social enterprises. He saw the opportunity to address the inequalities he had been campaigning against for years.

His bid was successful and 'Open Doors' established as social enterprise. Based in Grimsby, it provides healthcare, social support and hope to vulnerable people. Services range from acupuncture to anger management.

How much of a social entrepreneur are you?

Here is a quick test to help you work out how much of a social entrepreneur you are. Think about the social or environmental issues you feel most strongly about. Choose ones you might act upon as a social entrepreneur. Then ask yourself:

To what extent to you agree with these statements?

Agree a lot – score 4
Disagree a lot – score 1

	1	2	3	4
I have a very clear vision of what I want to change in the world				
Injustices and inequalities make me angry				
I want to be in control of my own income				
I am not afraid of hard work				
I don't mind standing out from the crowd				
I am determined to earn the money I need and not rely on grants				
TOTALS				

How did you score?

18-24 You have strong views and are determined. Don't let the mission detract from the need to be profitable too. Profit gives you choice – and means you survive.

12-18 You know your mind and balance your passion with perhaps a little pragmatism. You want to succeed and will compromise a little if needs be.

4-12 Social enterprise might be quite new to you and you're reading this book to find out more. Try the test again later and see how your confidence has grown.

Challenge your limits

Deep down we all know our limitations; or at least we think we do. They're the things we avoid doing because we've had a bad experience, or been told by others that it's not somewhere we should go. But people change over time and what you might have found challenging once, may not be anywhere near as daunting today.

You can't remember learning to walk, but you did. Now you probably take it for granted, that is unless illness or injury has made it difficult for you. A young child learning to walk falls over frequently. The same is true of almost anything else you learn as you go through life.

Practice makes perfect

In his book '*Outliers*' Malcolm Gladwell suggests that to become really good at anything, you need to practice for 10 000 hours. He cites the example of the Beatles, who played a Hamburg night club six nights a week before making it into the big time. They worked at what they did until they became expert. You can do the same.

Just as the toddler practices walking until it becomes automatic, so can you practice doing the things you know are holding you back. It's probably the only way to get better at them.

You also have to accept that you will change quicker than many people will notice. They will always remember as you were, not as you are. That's what makes the proverb; 'You're never a prophet in your own land' so true.

Heroes

We all have heroes, people we admire and aspire to be like. Athletes, TV celebrities and perhaps as social entrepreneurs, some of the great social reformers from history.

You can learn a lot from heroes, particularly if you research their life stories. Here are some things you might do:

→ Understand what prompted your heroes to do what they did. What is driving you in the direction you're heading? What lessons can you learn from your heroes?

→ Benchmark your life against theirs. Few were famous in childhood and many only achieved recognition late in life. What were your heroes doing at the age you are now? Chart your progress against theirs.

→ Spot the defining influences on your heroes' lives. How did these things happen? What can you do to bring about similar positive influences in your life?

Self-limiting beliefs

We all have self-limiting beliefs. That's because we know ourselves very well. We are well aware of what we're bad at and what others do well. The reason we compare ourselves against others is described earlier in this chapter. As a social entrepreneur, you need to challenge your self-limiting beliefs and gain the courage to do what you feel deep inside has to be done.

Many social entrepreneurs are motivated by an urge to help vulnerable people. If this is you, perhaps you have added incentive to work on your own perceptions and personal challenges.

Here are some questions to ask yourself. They'll help you conquer self-limiting beliefs. Start with something you need to do better to succeed as a social entrepreneur:

Task	Example answer	Your answer
Write down what you feel you can't do.	I cannot do public speaking.	
Write down why.	People will laugh and I'll dry up.	
Write down the opposite belief.	I'm a great public speaker.	
Describe why this might be true.	I make people think and tell good jokes.	
Describe how this changes your behaviour.	I'm quick to volunteer to talk about our work to groups.	

You next need to practice doing it. But don't set yourself up to fail. Start small and in a safe place, where people will be on your side. Then keep doing it until it becomes second nature.

Don't let others hold you back

It is always flattering to be described as a social entrepreneur. It means your commitment to each of those three key elements, people, profit and planet has been recognised. Paradoxically, by putting the needs of others at the top of their agenda, social entrepreneurs often become more successful themselves.

Above all, most would recognise social entrepreneurs as realists. People committed to making a difference in a way that is sustainable. That means sustainable for themselves as well as for those they are setting out to support.

However, people often have quite different views of what actually constitutes a social entrepreneur. Make comparisons to help people understand. The process enables both them and you to see more clearly the differences. For example:

Business person	Social entrepreneur	Campaigner
Profit at any cost	Sustainable change	Change at any cost
Money for self	Money for others	Others' money for others
May exploit the weak	Strengthens the weak	Champions the weak

Not everyone sees the point of social entrepreneurship:

➡ Some business people will criticise you for diluting your focus to make a difference as well as a profit.

➡ Some campaigners will criticise you for dirtying your campaign by adding income generation.

➡ Both might ask how you can reconcile making money for yourself whilst also being committed to helping others.

To many people, social enterprise and social entrepreneurship are new concepts. As with anything new, you find some eager to explore and experiment and others quick to criticise and condemn. Remember it is human nature to shoot down the things you cannot, or have chosen not to understand.

For example:

- In 1943, Thomas Watson, Chairman of IBM said; 'I think there is a world market for maybe five computers.'
- In 1927, HM Warner of Warner Brothers said; 'Who the hell wants to hear actors talk?'
- In 1962, Fred Smith, founder of FedEx wrote a paper outlining his business idea for overnight delivery when a student at Yale. His professor wrote; 'The concept is interesting and well-formed, but in order to earn better than a 'C,' the idea must be feasible.'

When people are critical of your plans as a social entrepreneur, remind them that in time, they might look back and realise that their comments look as silly with hindsight as these.

You know how you work best

As a social entrepreneur by definition you take greater responsibility for your actions. One benefit of this is you can choose to work in ways that suit your style and temperament. Those you choose to work with (as well indeed as those who choose to work with you) will be in part determined by your work style.

Autocratic – You like to call the shots. You know what you want to achieve and want to make the decisions. You might well listen to what others say, but in the end you do what you believe to be right. You make a great pioneer, breaking new ground.

Good points	Things to watch
Makes decisions quickly	May not always make the best decisions
Focused and assertive	Others may feel left out
Good in a crisis	May ignore opportunities

Democratic – You prefer consensus to making up your mind on your own. You like to listen to and involve others. Your mind can be changed by the majority view. You lead from within the team, instead of being out front. You listen as you lead and will do well leading an existing team into social enterprise.

Good points	Things to watch
Makes considered decisions	May consult too widely
Tolerant and understanding	Consultation takes time
May hesitate in a crisis	Needs structure

Paternalistic – You may be autocratic or democratic, but you have the best interests of your team at heart. You are concerned about the whole person, not just how they work with you. You listen to everyone and like to be liked. You have the empathy and patience to step into a new role, leading an existing team onto even greater things.

Good points	Things to watch
Good to work with	Might assume (s)he knows best
Caring towards colleagues & clients	Slow making tough decisions
Good communicator	May get distracted from the job in hand

Which of these resonates most with you? Are you someone who likes to do things your way, or do you like to consult with others? Perhaps you are a people person but maybe you are not. Don't try to change the way you are. Instead consider changing where you are. Work to your strengths and work in a way that suits your natural style.

In summary

- You are unique and should choose to do things that suit you.
- We all define who and what we are by those around us.
- Successful people know themselves very well.
- If you want to be a social entrepreneur you probably can.
- Practice makes perfect so practice a lot and don't give up.
- Challenge self-limiting beliefs, slowly but surely.
- Work in a way that suits your style.

Find out more

Kids Company	kidsco.org.uk
Andy's Kars	andys-kars.co.uk
Open Doors	thebiglifegroup.com/open-door

4

What You Are Going to Change in the World

'The danger of the past was that men became slaves. The danger of the future is that men become robots.'

Erich Fromm – *The Sane Society*, 1955

Passion from your past

We all have a past, present and future. Our past has made us who we are. Our present is where we are and the future offers promise of what we might become. Often it is events and experiences from our past that give us the drive and focus to become social entrepreneurs.

Bob Geldof describes how losing his mother to a sudden brain haemorrhage when he was seven taught him what he described as; 'the hardest lesson of all, that life is unfair'. Much later he was spurred into action by a TV documentary about the 1984 famine in Ethiopia. It was a time when European farmers were being paid subsidies to grow surplus food that was then stored and destroyed. This seemingly unjust imbalance, with people starving on one continent whilst nearby, food was being wasted prompted Geldof to start 'Live Aid'. The first Live Aid concert is said to have raised more than £40m for famine relief.

As a popular performer, Geldof was sufficiently in the public eye, with access to other performers, broadcasters and media to organise Live Aid. Few of us have similar opportunity to make a difference on such a scale.

Dee Dawson was a 42 year old mother of four, with another child on the way and had just qualified as a doctor. She also had an MBA and an interest in anorexia. She was not sure what she wanted to do next. Then her husband's business suddenly collapsed and the family was without income.

Realising that she would need time to recover from the shock Dee looked objectively at what the family had and could do. They owned their house and she was a qualified doctor. She decided to open her house as a clinic for young anorexics. She reckoned that as the house and her time were their main assets, she had little to lose and everything to gain.

Today Rhodes Farm is a successful enterprise that has helped countless youngsters recover from anorexia. Dee is making money and changing the world.

Exploring your past

You don't have to have experienced something unpleasant to feel driven to change the world. But you do need to have something you feel strongly enough about. Often it will be a blend of your past experiences and current situation that combine to create your opportunity. Geldof was sensitised to life's unfairness by the death of his mother. He was moved to do something by a TV documentary.

It can be difficult finding the right thing for you to do. No one person can change the whole world; it is simply too vast and complex. What you have to do is to find something very specific that you can:

➡ feel very passionate about;
➡ believe you can do something about;
➡ make the change you create lasting and self sustaining.

Good social entrepreneurs always recognise the vital importance of that last point. To bring about change that does not last can actually be counter productive. You raise hopes and expectations only for them to be dashed. This point can be illustrated by the soup kitchen argument.

The soup kitchen argument

If you set up a soup kitchen for homeless people, many will come for the comfort, warmth and food it provides. Life will be more tolerable and the incentive to escape street life lower. If the soup kitchen closes, those who became dependent on it find themselves worse off than they were to start with.

Spend the same money and effort in helping homeless people regain confidence, learn new skills and find work, perhaps in a hotel kitchen, and you have created change that becomes self sustaining. Creating dependency helps no one.

Here are some questions to ask yourself about your past. Consider them carefully and perhaps discuss with family and friends. Find the passion from your past and you might find your opportunity for the future:

1. What is your earliest memory? How did that experience shape the person you are today?
2. What within your family or cultural history has most shaped your attitudes and beliefs?
3. What have you experienced or witnessed that has really made you stop and think?
4. What led you to follow the education and career path you have chosen?
5. What triggered you to buy this book? How does it relate to your answers to the first four questions?

Somewhere within what you think, discuss and write down will be the seed from which you are growing as a social entrepreneur.

Ambition for your future

Most of us have travelled on a plane. Can you remember the safety briefing the cabin crew give before take off? It contains a powerful metaphor that applies to every social entrepreneur or social enterprise.

When demonstrating how the oxygen masks fall from the above your head if cabin pressure drops, the crew always tell you this; 'if you're travelling with a child, put your mask on before you fit theirs.' Why do they tell you to do this? It's because you might lose consciousness whilst fitting your child's mask if you have not fitted your own first. Your instinct is to protect your child before yourself. Logic says that if you do, both of you are exposed to greater risk. Social enterprise is just the same. Only by protecting yourself can you be sure of your ability to help others.

Take the soup kitchen example. The homeless people become dependent on the soup kitchen and those running the operation on charitable donations. As a social entrepreneur, you need to make sure that what you start looks after itself first, because only then can it look after those less able with any reliability.

This might contrast with your experience if you've arrived at social enterprise from a charity background. That's because charities focus on generating sufficient donations to meet the need. As that becomes harder, earning income through enterprising activity becomes both more appealing and more important.

And yes, as you will see in later chapters, one of the arts of social enterprise is to sell tangible outcomes to funders, as well as engage in commercial activity.

Your future

There are some basics about personal ambition that every entrepreneur has to consider when starting out. Being a social entrepreneur is in this respect no different. Here are some of them:

▸ **Lifestyle** – What do you want your life to look like? How do you want to spend your time? Where do you want to be and who do you want to spend time with? Consider all of these points. One benefit of being an entrepreneur is that you can make choices.

▸ **Wealth** – It is unlikely you will become hugely wealthy as a social entrepreneur, but wealth is relative. You do need to make sure you earn a reasonable living and have money to set aside for your future. Work out what you need and don't be embarrassed about setting out to earn it.

▸ **Family** – If you have a partner and perhaps children, you need to factor their needs into your plan. It would be wrong to sacrifice the security and opportunity of those you love. However, it's as likely they share your passion so do involve them in your plans.

▸ **Health** – Entrepreneurial success takes stamina, grit and determination. You need to be realistic about both your physical and mental health. If you start a social enterprise, it will be dependent on your initiative, energy and enthusiasm. You need to make sure you work in a way that doesn't make you ill.

Remember that once you've made the commitment to start, it might be years before you can safely step back and let others take the lead. What you do has to be right for you. Don't become a martyr to a cause for which you will lose enthusiasm. That does no one any favours.

Tahir Hussain was born in Pakistan but raised in Peterborough. Tahir did well at school and became an industrial chemist. He married and had children, but in time became disillusioned with corporate life. He wanted something more fulfilling but was unsure what to do.

His parents played key roles within the local Asian community so Tahir was aware that immigrant kids often struggle at school. For many years he voluntarily helped Asian youngsters with their science homework. He also realised how lucky he was that he had done well and that his own children were doing the same.

He saw the opportunity to create a social enterprise that provides affordable or free extra tuition for kids getting behind with their homework. IQ Plus was established and quickly became popular. However, he found that those with the greatest need could not afford even his modest fees. He took business advice and incorporated the business as a Community Interest Company. This enabled him to seek grants from agencies funded to raise educational attainment in his city. He became a social entrepreneur.

As a social entrepreneur, you have to follow your own dream, not the dreams of others who lack the courage to do it themselves.

Where are you now?

Pause for a moment and reflect on your day to day life. What are the issues that most concern you and why? How do these resonate with your past experience, your upbringing or your personal values? As a social entrepreneur you will be most effective if the changes you want to make in the world are to things you are currently experiencing or witnessing. Ask yourself:

➡ What has recently made you feel indignant and why?

➡ Who did you encounter that most aroused your sense of social injustice?

➡ Where did you go that made you most excited about your future potential?

Answering these questions and extending the thought processes they provoke will take you closer to defining your vision and aspirations as a social entrepreneur.

Your campaigning style

All social entrepreneurs are campaigners to some extent; it's how they get things done. Campaigning is all about persuading people to support a cause or point of view. Campaigners champion the cause they believe. Their belief, passion and strength of argument changes minds and win support.

How you campaign will depend largely on your personal style. Some people are more extrovert than others. That said, sometimes the most timid people can find previously untapped reserves of self confidence when lobbying and campaigning for something they wholeheartedly believe to be right.

You need to find which aspects of campaigning best suited your personal style. This is because if you do things in the way you find most comfortable, you will be able to achieve more. Although never underestimate your ability to surprise yourself – passion for your cause takes over!

Campaigning demands a number of skills; which of these do you find easiest?

➡ **Researching** the issues and making sure you know the full story.

→ **Exploring** and evaluating opportunities so that you make the best choices.
→ **Identifying** the people best able to support and perhaps fund you.
→ **Influencing** people through publicity, promotion and face to face selling.

Once you have a better grasp of how you campaign best, you can gain a clearer idea of *what* you can do best. In other words, different campaigning styles lend themselves to different kinds of social entrepreneurship, For example:

→ **Researchers** are good at putting together reasoned arguments that change behaviours and practices. If you are a natural researcher, you might find it easier to lobby others rather than lead the change yourself.
→ **Explorers** are out there in the thick of things. They win support by shouting loudly from the front line, demanding attention and support. Are you an extrovert explorer? In which case you'll probably lead from the front line.
→ **Identifiers** are more subtle, digging out the people they need to influence and working on them individually. They succeed by stealth and can be very effective. If this is you, you can change a lot but might not get the credit.
→ **Influencers** are like loud-hailers, magnifying what others have persuaded them are good things to promote. They may not do detail or subtlety, but they usually get noticed. If this is you, spare some of the credit for those who prepared the way.

You may find it strange that campaigning is compared with selling. As you'll find later (in Chapter 10) selling is a key skill for any social entrepreneur. However, selling in this context is often a very subtle rather than a pushy process.

In fact as a social entrepreneur, you can learn a lot from how some of the world's most successful campaigners operated. Read each of the following examples and see which you would have found easiest to do had you been in their shoes:

Martin Luther King was one of the most respected leaders of the American Civil Rights Movement. He is best remembered for the many rousing speeches he wrote and delivered.

Mahatma Gandhi trained as a barrister but advocated non-cooperation, non-resistance and non-violence as the most effective ways to campaign.

Rachel Carson was a scientist and perhaps one of the world's first environmental campaigners. She raised awareness of pesticide poisoning and contamination by writing letters to national newspapers.

Each of these worked in ways they felt comfortable. Each was also very effective.

Managing your enthusiasm and expectations

Not everyone sees the world as you do. More importantly, they may not attach the same significance to things you consider to be of vital importance. This can be very frustrating because when you're passionate about something, you quite naturally want others to be as well.

The danger is that as you push ahead on your agenda, the issues others feel are equally important might get left behind. It's like taking a school party to the zoo. You love the elephants and the spiders frighten you. The group finds itself watching the elephants being fed, playing and even sleeping. Time runs out before your group reaches the spiders. You've had a great day but notice some seem miserable. It might be because they love spiders and feel short-changed.

Your ability to see and value other people's perspectives and priorities will help you win their support.

> 'The whole problem with the world is that fools and fanatics are always so certain of themselves, but wiser people so full of doubts.'
>
> Bertrand Russell

 What works

It's OK to be enthusiastic and passionate but don't cross the line and be considered a fanatic.

How to be realistic

There is no such thing as right or wrong when it comes to measuring aspiration. Some people want to create vast organisations and others are content to work on a smaller scale, keeping in touch with the grassroots of the social or environmental issues they feel strongly about.

Here are some points to consider as you reflect on what you want to achieve and decide realistically, how ambitious you really are:

→ **Size** – Your ambition might be to create a global aid agency. Alternatively you might just want to save your local community centre. To the individual beneficiary, each might be of equal significance. Clearly the aid agency has a greater total impact, but that does not make it better or more worthwhile. Size doesn't matter.

→ **Starting point** – Bob Geldof created 'Live Aid' when already globally known as a pop singer. Your starting point is probably more modest and so too will be what you can initially achieve. You have to start from where you are.

→ **Resources** – Are you investing your own money or applying for grants? Perhaps you will borrow too. It's important to plan within the bounds of what resources you can acquire. You have to be realistic.

→ **Knowledge and skill** – There will be lots you realise you don't know. There will also be plenty you don't yet appreciate that you don't know. Growing anything, especially growing yourself, takes time and involves a lot of learning. You have to start where you are.

Your long-term goals will certainly help you plan. Your short-term goals will make sure you survive and thrive along the way. It is true to say that almost all large organisations were once very small ones. You have to start where you are right now.

In summary

🐣 You are unique and should choose to do things that suit you.

🐣 We all define who and what we are by those around us.

🐣 Successful people know themselves very well.

🐣 If you want to be a social entrepreneur you probably can.

🐣 Practice makes perfect so practice a lot and don't give up.

🐣 Challenge self-limiting beliefs, slowly but surely.

🐣 Work in a way that suits your style.

🐣 Ambition is good, but be realistic too.

Find out more

Live Aid	bobgeldof.info/Charity/liveaid.html
Rhodes Farm	rhodesfarm.com
IQ Plus Tuition Services	iqplus.co.uk

5

Explore Your Entrepreneurial Style

'So little done, so much to do'

Cecil Rhodes, speaking on the day he died, 1902

Your starting point

Y ou don't have to start your own organisation to be a social entrepreneur. There are many ways you can be a very successful social entrepreneur. It's simply a matter of finding the right way for you.

Too many people go off to find their destiny only to discover it back where their search began. It can be very tempting to walk away from where you are to create something new. As a social entrepreneur you have to rise above the instinctive response and do what's going to make the biggest difference. Start with what you have, then look at the alternatives.

Within an organisation

Many successful social entrepreneurs operate within an existing organisation. It can be a very good starting point, if only because you have existing resources you can focus in a new direction.

Lance Gardner, mentioned in Chapter 3 is a good example. He set up the very successful Open Doors project in Grimsby within the existing structure of the NHS. He could have resigned from his job, raised the cash he needed and set up an independent organisation. He didn't do this because he didn't need to. You might describe him as a social Intrapreneur.

> **Intrapreneur:** an employee of a large corporation who is given freedom and financial support to create new products, services, systems, etc., and does not have to follow the corporation's usual routines or protocols.

Social Intrapreneur is a phrase likely to become more widely known as the impact and value of social entrepreneurship within organisations becomes more widely appreciated. People have talked about intrapreneurship for the past 30 years. It is a recognised way to encourage innovation within large organisations. The social Intrapreneur is someone who takes the initiative and boosts his or her employer's social or environmental impact in a financially sustainable way.

Benefits of working within an organisation

→ You have a job and so don't need to worry about personal income.
→ There are existing resources you can use and people around to help you.
→ Your organisation has suppliers, customers and momentum.
→ There is potential to make a big difference and grow your concept internally.

Drawbacks

→ You have to do a job as well so things might take longer than you'd like.
→ You might be competing for people's time and attention with other projects.
→ Commitment to your project might be patchy, creating barriers to progress at times.
→ Your timetable might be compromised to meet more commercial company objectives.

Benefits to the organisation

→ Retains innovative people who otherwise would leave and go it alone.

➡ Can show that it cares about people and planet as well as profit.
➡ Sustainable and authentic 'home grown' social responsibility.

How to find social intrapreneurs in an organisation

One way you can be intrapreneurial is to help people within your organisation focus and realise their intrapreneurial dreams. In fact if you are a frustrated social Intrapreneur yourself, encouraging your employer to do some of these things will make life a lot easier for you. It might also encourage others to step forward, giving you a peer group of like minded people to work with.

➡ **Competition** – arrange an open competition that employees can enter. The winning project should be chosen for its ability to benefit the organisation as well as the difference it is likely to make to others. The prize could be a budget, support and some time away from your current job to develop the idea.
➡ **Café** – bring in some social enterprise advisers and other experts in the field you want to encourage people to explore. Stage a drop-in café style 'ideas surgery' and encourage people to share their ideas.
➡ **Pre-retirees** – in the last year of someone's career they often find their operational responsibilities reduce. This can give them time to develop entrepreneurial new projects that can be incubated by the organisation and then grown by the individual when they leave. Use pre-retirement workshops to help people create socially responsible

projects that give them a lasting interest and the organisation measurable payback.

Increasingly, organisations that strive to deliver a 'triple bottom line' outperform those that focus on profit alone.

Andreas Eggenberg of Amanco, a pipe maker for the construction industry in Central America developed an affordable irrigation system that increased productivity and income on some of Guatamala's poorest farms. As the farmers prospered, they were able to buy more sophisticated equipment from Amanco. By working as an Intrapreneur Eggenberg helped farmers out of poverty and created a new market for his company's products.

By inspiring others to start organisations

Just as you can be a social Intrapreneur, creating a difference within an organisation, so too can you encourage others to start organisations. Entrepreneurs in general are better at starting new things. Other people may be less inventive but far better able to maintain and build organisations that last.

Often, the most successful social entrepreneurs are those who encourage others to start things. They may well do the initial campaigning and bring together the right people, then hand over to those with the expertise to build and sustain what results.

Social entrepreneurs are people who can see new solutions to old problems. They know what needs to be done, but not necessarily how to do it.

A common metaphor used to describe people who do this is to compare them to 'the grit in an oyster.' That's because pearls are the result of the oyster's reaction to a potentially harmful irritant. In fact it is more usually a microscopic parasite than a piece of grit that prompts the oyster's defence mechanisms to surround it with a pearl. Just as pearls are created by something very small, so too can one person prompt the creation of a very large organisation.

> 'It is a vital ingredient in life to receive a "golden seed" early on from someone you respect, a compliment or expression of confidence in you that fortifies self-belief.'
>
> Charles Handy, 2001

As Charles Handy suggests, sometimes all you have to do is tell someone that what they see as impossible, can be done. Handy calls this sowing the golden seed.

Benefits of inspiring others to start an organisation

→ You don't lose sight of the big picture.
→ It's really rewarding helping others succeed.
→ You don't find yourself drowning in difficult detail.
→ You can move on when it's running smoothly.

Drawbacks

→ You may have to compromise your vision so that others will buy in.
→ It will not be seen as 'your' project; others will rightly get the credit.

→ The organisation will probably not provide you with income.

→ You might find it difficult to walk away, even though you must.

Reed Paget was a journalist. He saw first-hand the impact of consumerism and waste around the world. He set up Belu Water, the UK's first 'carbon neutral' bottled water brand. Belu Water produces products in glass bottles as well as from compostable plastic made from corn starch. All Belu's profits are used to fund clean water projects around the world.

Paget was inspired to start Belu when he heard United Nations Secretary-General Kofi Annan launch the UN Global Compact in 2001. This initiative 'uses capitalism to change the world.' Belu is a commercial business, but its profits are invested in making a difference.

Kofi Annan inspired Reed Paget to create his social enterprise. The success of Belu Water's environmental credentials (Belu is the first of 70 000 'carbon neutral' products to be stocked by Tesco), has prompted numerous other bottled water brands to work towards carbon neutrality.

One speech inspired Reed Paget; one small company has changed the bottled water industry. It's how lasting social and environmental change is delivered.

With your own social enterprise

The most visible social entrepreneurs are those who start their own social enterprises. So far we have looked at social entrepreneurship as an attitude, mindset or philosophy. From here on, the focus is on social enterprise. So why start your own social enterprise?

Benefits of starting your own organisation

→ You follow your passion and literally become the change you want to see.

→ You can strike your own balance between people, planet and profit.

→ Starting a business, like becoming a parent, can be hugely satisfying.

→ You can recruit people with skills that complement your own.

Drawbacks

→ It's a big commitment, emotionally, intellectually and usually financially.

→ You can't start something and then walk away. You need to see it through.

→ Running an organisation can take you away from campaigning.

→ You might find it difficult to let go and delegate.

If you're planning to start your own social enterprise, or build on one that's already established, remember not to judge all social enterprises equally. Those started by a passionate social entrepreneur will be very different from those started by people who are competent managers, but not entrepreneurs.

In other words, if you have confidence in your abilities and passion for your cause, together with a willingness to seek and listen to advice, you will probably succeed. If you're running a social enterprise because circumstances have thrust you into that role, the harsh reality is that you might not. That is, unless you recognise the strengths and weaknesses of both yourself and your organisation and act to plug any gaps.

A reality check

Finally, before leaving this section of the book, which is all about you, take a reality check before going any further. You need to be sure that what you are doing or planning to do is going to:

➡ meet what you and others view as a genuine social or environmental need;

➡ be innovative and clearly fill a gap in the marketplace;

➡ be sustainable and flexible enough to adapt to changing needs.

Andrew Mawson arrived in Bromley-by-Bow as the new minister of a local church. He found largely underused church buildings and a massive need for community facilities within his parish. What followed grew to become one of the most successful social enterprises in London. Mawson started the Bromley-by-Bow Centre, using his church as the starting point for a massive regeneration project, including the UK's first 'Healthy Living Centre'.

He attributes the success of this venture to his decision to listen to and then encourage and support local people to get involved. He reckoned that they knew better than the visiting officials what was needed in their community.

In summary

🥚 You can be a social entrepreneur by changing the organisation you work for, inspiring others to start or by starting something yourself.

🥚 How you can most make a difference depends on where you are right now.

🥚 You can inspire others simply by speaking your mind.

🥚 Small actions can have large consequences. Think big!

🥚 Don't pre-judge your chances of success by comparing yourself with others less passionate than you. Look for differences as well as similarities.

Find out more

Belu Water	belu.org
United Nation's Global Compact	unglobalcompact.org

Part Three

How to Start

6

Organisations and How to Start Them

'Whenever a man does a thoroughly stupid thing, it is always from the noblest motives.'

Oscar Wilde – The Picture of Dorian Gray, 1891

Defining vision, mission and values

It would be stupid to start anything without clear measurable objectives. It would also be remarkably easy. You see an immediate need or a gross injustice and are moved to act. Your response is emotional and rightly so. But to create a sustainable social enterprise, you need logic and reason as well as emotion. Most of us would jump into a lake to save a drowning child, but creating a water safety programme for schools needs more thinking through.

Many are moved to become social entrepreneurs by personal experience. Having saved one drowning child you vow to find a way to stop similar accidents happening in the future. But just as you leap into the water on impulse, creating an organisation needs more thinking. This section of the book tells you how. Although each chapter assumes you are going to do this yourself, don't worry, you won't be able to do everything yourself, so share the tasks and enjoy the journey.

Vision

To share your vision with others you need to write it down. To do that you need to be able to define it clearly using words others will understand. For example, to continue the analogy above, let's assume you have indeed saved a drowning child and want to reduce the risk of future similar incidents. You want to provide swimming and water safety training to youngsters at school. To make this affordable, perhaps even free to schools, you need to generate income in other ways. But that's how not what.

You might summarise your vision as: 'To create a world in which every child feels confident in water.' The sentence says what you want to achieve without being specific about how. That's OK because you can have a vision without any idea how to achieve it. However, it is conceivably achievable and that's important.

An unrealistic vision, for example: 'to conquer death and achieve immortality for all.' Might be a nice idea but in reality impossible to ever achieve. We all know that one day we will die and that knowledge destroys any credibility the vision might hold. People will not support trying to achieve the impossible.

So your very first step in converting your passion into action is to define your vision. You can't change the whole world, so you need to define the elements you feel most strongly about and perhaps (but not necessarily) have some relevant experience or skill that will help you realise your vision, at least in part.

Exercise

It would be a good idea to write yourself a vision statement. It needs to be:

- **Specific** – addressing one issue, need or community.
- **Bold** – and cannot be delivered quickly.
- **Feasible** – because people have to believe it can somehow be achieved.

You might find it helpful to put a timeframe to your vision. When you achieve it, you can always write another one! For example:

'By 2015 our Women's Centre will be the city's largest and most popular provider of advice, training and encouragement to women seeking to improve their lives and their opportunities.'

You can see that this example is SPECIFIC in defining, what, where and when. It is also BOLD as it seeks to be both the largest and most popular. Lastly it is FEASIBLE because you limits its ambition to one group in one place. National domination would probably not be feasible.

Now write your vision statement and ask a friend or colleague to check that it is Specific, Bold and Feasible.

Mission

You have defined your vision and now have to work out how. This is where you bring the vision into focus by writing down your mission. Your mission statement has to be short, specific and measurable. It expands on your vision statement, telling the reader how you plan to deliver the change you have decided you want to see.

Let's return to the example of a vision we've used already. You want to make children confident in water. There are many ways you could seek to prevent accidental drownings. You could consider:

➡ providing warning notices beside rivers, canals, ponds and on beaches;
➡ creating advice posters and DVDs to raise awareness of the danger;
➡ funding swimming and lifesaving classes for children.

Your vision statement contains the clue as to which option you favour. Only training will make children more confident around water. Warning signs and alarming posters will raise awareness of the danger, but also increase fear should a child find themselves in the water unexpectedly.

Your mission statement then might be: 'we recruit, train and support volunteer swimming coaches who we place in schools to teach basic lifesaving skills to children and their teachers.'

Now you have said exactly what you are going to do. This means that others can see how they can help.

Exercise

Write yourself a mission statement that says:

* **What** – you are going to do.
* **Who** – is going to do it.
* **How** – it be achieved.

The mission statement needs to mean something to you and everyone who comes into contact with your organisation. For example:

'City Women's Centre brings together the most inspirational tutors, advisers and counsellors. Together they deliver personalised programmes that help women set goals and develop the skills they need to achieve them.'

You can see that this example explains WHO is going to do the work and HOW they are going to do it. It also makes it very clear WHAT is going to happen. The emphasis on inspiration is crucial as in this example it is probably the single most important quality of the project.

Values

All organisations have values. As a social entrepreneur yours will be both important and wholesome. After all, your personal goal is to create positive change for others, as well as yourself.

Most large organisations display their values. If they have a strong service element to their business, their values might be posted all over the place, for example on the wall behind a reception desk and in other places customers look. Others simply publish them on their company website, in their annual report and in their employee handbook. Values are very important to staff. They have to work by them and many will define the quality of the relationship they have with their employer.

Values are usually linked to the organisation's philosophy. They may cover things such as quality, integrity, efficiency and excellence. The problem is that too often they are written by committee and end up as bland statements that could apply to any organisation. They then become worthy but with little real credibility.

For example, you could say:

'We will always act with integrity and honesty, never compromising our clients in any way.'

Alternatively, you could make the statement more accountable:

'We will never take money from or work with any organisation that demands we compromise our clients in any way, however small.'

You don't need to use words like integrity and honesty because alone they say little. Instead use words that define how you will work with integrity and let the reader interpret in their own way.

Exercise

Write yourself value statements that are:

- **Measurable** – so that others can hold you accountable.
- **Appropriate** – to the organisation you are and the work you do.
- **Simple** – using words that everyone will readily understand.

Assessing the potential

For your social enterprise to grow and become self-sufficient, there has to be sufficient need and demand for the services it will provide. There is a subtle but vital difference between need and demand that you need to fully understand.

- **Need** – can be defined as an 'urgent want'. It's something that should be done, that people will welcome being done and above all, something that fits with your vision of the future you want to create.
- **Demand** – can be defined as being wanted for purchase. Demand is what people will pay for.

In a purely for profit enterprise, demand is more important than need. For example, people:

→ **Need** to drink to survive. Water alone can meet this need and in most of the world, is freely available.
→ **Demand** and pay for colas, beer, tea and coffee. They don't need them but choose (or are persuaded by marketers) to demand and pay for them.

Charities raise money to meet needs where there may be no demand. Famine relief at a time of drought is a crucial need. But the starving people cannot buy food so there is no demand. If you opened a Tesco supermarket in an African refugee camp no one would shop there. So charities raise money from people concerned about others in need, then spend it meeting that need.

What works

The more successfully you can align demand with need, the more sustainable your social enterprise will become.

Take, for example, a community café. It may have been established to provide a meeting place in a deprived community. People use the café because it's a good place to meet friends or just stave off loneliness. It's on a large housing estate with no competition. To visit other cafes, people have to travel into town.

The café meets both needs and demands.

Needs:

→ A place to drop in and make or meet friends.
→ Work experience opportunities for local jobseekers.
→ Local people needed somewhere to meet friends.

Demands:

→ The local regeneration company wanted to fund a meeting place.
→ An employment charity had funding to provide work placements.
→ Local people were willing to spend money in a local café.

The café has two distinct customer groups; organisations working to make the area a better place to live and work and local people with nowhere to meet. Starbucks would be unlikely to invest in opening a café on a run-down estate and people there would be unwilling to pay high prices for coffee and snacks. Starbucks as a 'for profit' business invest where they believe they can get the greatest return.

However, as a social enterprise, run for the benefit of the community, the business model is quite different. Grant funding helps cover the set up costs. Training subsidies help the long-term unemployed gain work experience and because overheads are lower and there's no capital loan to repay, the coffee and sandwiches are affordable by local people.

Assessing the potential for a social enterprise is therefore less straightforward than it is for an enterprise focused on profit alone. To check out the potential of your idea you need to work out:

➡ **How big** is the issue? Is it local, regional, national or global? (If local, what can you learn from similar projects elsewhere?).

➡ **How long** will it last? (There will always be poverty; natural disasters come and go).

➡ **Who cares** most about solving things? How can they help you and how can you help them?

➡ **Who gains from fixing the problem** as well as those directly affected? (For example, reducing worklessness increases what is spent in local shops.)

Asking yourself these questions helps you put some scale to your project. Remember that size and scale are only problems if you estimate them incorrectly. You do not want to be swamped by demand; neither do you want to acquire expensive resources that are under-utilised.

> **!** **WARNING**
>
> Your research will often reveal very detailed strategy and research documents, usually written by consultants that define need and suggest what is required. Don't take their word for it; instead ask the people you are setting out to help. They will help you balance big picture statistics with grassroots reality.

Structures and how they can help or hinder

When you seek advice about how best to set up a social enterprise you inevitably get bogged down considering alternative legal structures. How you set your organisation up is important of course, but choosing the right structure should not precede writing the business plan. Only when you fully know how your organisation is going to operate can you really work out the best legal structure to adopt.

Choose a structure too early, and you can find yourself limited by rules and regulations. It might even be that you are already working within an organisation which is already appropriately structured to give you the freedom to be more entrepreneurial. A lot depends upon where you are coming from and the direction in which you want to head. Chapter 8 looks in some detail at the options but for now, here are some pointers to get you started.

At one end of the spectrum you will find the:

Registered Charity

Every charity is different with their 'memo & arts' defining what they can do, where and for whom. If you currently work within a charity and want to set up a social enterprise, you usually can without creating a new organisation. Most charities are permitted to trade in a modest way. It might make sense to do this initially and then separate your social enterprise when it starts to grow.

And at the other, the:

Limited Company

The most common form of registered business is the limited liability company. The limited liability simply means that the company has a separate legal identity to its owners or the directors who manage it. Usually the company is 'limited by share', which means the owners have invested what is called share capital. This is the money they are risking because it is lost if the business fails. Equally it earns dividends if the company is profitable. These are distributed to the shareholders.

A limited company can be a social enterprise, as indeed can any organisation. However, as most limited companies are 'for profit' so you may have to work hard to demonstrate you are a social enterprise.

Bridging the gap are two different structures:

Community Interest Company

This is essentially a limited company with some bolt-on sections within its memo & arts. These define the proportion of the profits that must be invested in supporting those the organisation was set up to help. This group literally forms the 'community of interest'. Private and organisational shareholders can receive the remaining profits as dividends. Share value growth is capped and assets acquired remain 'locked' within the business. The memo & arts also names the charity or community organisation to which the assets are bequeathed in the event of the enterprise failing.

Industrial and Provident Society

Many cooperatives, clubs and associations are set up in this way. Shares are issued and sold and dividends may be paid to the shareholders. Unlike a limited company, the shareholders in an IPS are usually its members, employees or customers. It is a form of public ownership and therefore trades exclusively for the benefit of its shareholders.

Communities raising money to buy land and buildings often use this vehicle to issue and sell shares. Unlike in a limited or public limited company, each shareholder has equal voting rights irrespective of the size of their shareholding.

Company Limited by Guarantee

These are limited liability companies without issued shares. Instead the owners, or members guarantee the business. In a limited by share company, each shareholder can lose their investment if the business fails. In a limited by guarantee company, each member's potential loss is capped at the limit of their guarantee. This is usually £1.

You might wonder why all companies are not limited by guarantee rather than share. The problem is that you need share capital to fund the business and match bank borrowings. A limited by guarantee company is less able to borrow, but conversely, because there is no profit distribution (no shareholders) grant makers will often give them money.

There are other forms too, with new ones coming along every year or two.

 What works

It'll be far easier to choose the right legal structure once you've written your business plan. The planning process will show you the right way to go.

Getting it right first time

As a social entrepreneur, perhaps setting up a social enterprise, what you do will always be more important than what you are. Creating an enterprise of any kind is like embarking on a journey. The route you take, as well as the vehicle you might use, will depend on your preference, your budget and your destination.

As your journey gets underway, you make choices and compromises. Taking a train is faster than walking, but you lose the freedom to stop and start whenever you like. A car can be as fast as a train, gives you more flexibility, but costs more to hire than a train ticket. And if your journey is short, why not walk anyway?

Having defined your vision and mission, you will now have a better idea of what your journey needs to look like. You have also, earlier in this chapter, explored your values. You've considered both your personal ones and those your organisation will embrace. These too might dictate the speed and style of your enterprise journey. For example, it might be appropriate to complete the journey more slowly, but in a way with a lower environmental impact.

Taking advice

It makes sense to complete this chapter with some tips on taking advice. The enterprise journey is an emotional one; social enterprise more so than most. You need to be emotionally involved in what you're planning to have the passion, conviction and determination you need to succeed. However, that emotional involvement can also cloud your objectivity and make you prone to making bad decisions. That's why advice can be useful.

Research shows that most people seek enterprise advice from people they know. Usually these are people they feel have some relevant expertise, perhaps they run an organisation themselves.

As you venture deeper into the world of social enterprise you will find specialist advisers able, not surprisingly to offer specialist advice. In the UK, the Social Enterprise Coalition website is a good place to start. Each UK region will have specialist social enterprise support organisations, often able to give free advice, at least initially. Business Link is a government funded agency with teams of advisers and useful helpline teams offering help over the phone. Last but not least, enterprise agencies are independent business advice agencies often social enterprises themselves. All are worth checking out.

When seeking and listening to advice always:

→ Ask professional advisers what experience they have of social enterprise – not all advisers do.
→ Explain your vision and describe what you want to achieve in both the short and the long term.
→ Listen to what is said and challenge anything you don't understand or agree with.
→ Accept that you and the adviser might have different views and opinions.
→ Reflect carefully and if needs be seek a second opinion before acting. Equally, don't ask everyone and delay doing anything; that's called procrastination!

In summary

- Vision is your image of the future you want to create.
- Mission is who, what and how you are going to do to realise the vision.
- Define your values using words that mean people can hold you accountable.
- You set out to meet needs, but only by satisfying demands do you get paid.
- Before you plan your venture, first check out the demand, now and in the future.
- Don't get hung up about legal structures until you have written your business plan.
- Always take advice but don't follow it unless it feels right.

Find out more

Belu Water   belu.org
Social Enterprise Coalition   socialenterprise.org.uk
Business Link   businesslink.gov.uk
Enterprise Agencies   nfea.com

7

Preparing a Business Plan That Covers All the Angles

'We are not in a position in which we have nothing to work with. We already have capacities, talents, direction, missions and callings.'

Abraham Maslow

What to include and why

Your business plan will define for you and others how you are going to turn your vision into reality. You know where you're starting from and where you want to end up. You also have a wealth of information, ideas and experience that could be summarised in your plan. So how much do you include? If you talk to most bank managers, they'll tell you they prefer a business plan that is short and to the point.

Short business plan	Long business plan
Gets the key points over quickly	The vision might be clouded by detail
Easy to remember the key points	Difficult to find the key points
All your own work so reflects your passion, style and priorities	Based on a downloaded template so might seem impersonal
A handy document you can refer to	A document no one reads

It is in many ways far harder to write a short business plan. The process forces you to summarise, to be concise and to focus on what is most important. The clarity you will gain by writing a short plan will make it far easier for you to explain your plans to others.

As well as being short, your business plan also needs to be:

→ Written in your own words – because then it's obvious you've written it and have ownership of what it says.
→ Jargon free – because you might show it to a funder or lender who doesn't understand the detail of your sector.
→ Well signposted – so the reader knows where they are.

→ Supplemented with relevant appendices – that provide more detail for readers who want more detail.

→ Supported with financial projections – that show how they will quickly become sustainable.

What works

The easier a business plan is to understand, the more people support it.

The social enterprise difference

If you were writing a business plan for a straightforward 'for profit' business, you would focus on:

→ the market you plan to serve and your position within it;
→ your product or service;
→ your qualifications and credibility in your marketplace;
→ how you will market your offer;
→ your financial goals, costs and cash flow;
→ how you will measure your performance;

As a social entrepreneur, you have more to consider and build in to your plan. Some will be dismissive of your social mission. To counter this you need to make it a pivotal aspect of your business plan. In other words, the closer you can get to making profit the product of your positive impact on people and planet the better.

The business plan for a social enterprise also has to include:

→ the social, community or environmental need being addressed;
→ why you are the right organisation to address it;

➡ the social impact and its value;

➡ how you will be financially sustainable.

Striking the balance between needs and wants

As you prepare your business plan you need to differentiate between things you need and things you want. This might be difficult if you are new to enterprise. If, for example, your history is within the public sector, you will be used to managing budgets, but not to starting from scratch. When you start any new venture, there are things you need and things you want.

Imagine you are starting a social enterprise café that will provide employment opportunities for people with additional needs:

➡ You **need** staff, customers and perhaps a contract to provide work experience.

➡ You **want** to rent premises, buy equipment and advertise.

But surely premises are vital you say? How can you run a café without space, tables and equipment? The fact is that you might want to create your own place from scratch, but you actually might be able to manage without the expense. For example:

➡ You could do a deal with a large employer, take over their staff canteen and find yourself with a ready to roll business, captive customers and a very affordable, low risk way to start.

➡ A local shopping centre could have just had a café go bust owing them rent. You could take over the place 'lock, stock and barrel' at a fraction of the cost of setting up from scratch.

➥ A commercial vehicle dealer might provide you with a mobile café that you can take to events. It could advertise the dealership and publicly demonstrate their commitment to making a difference.

You can see that lateral thinking is useful when you set up any enterprise, especially a social enterprise. It's easy to spend money and do things the conventional way. Indeed you will meet plenty of people eager to help.

Exercise

Create your own list of needs and wants.

Write down a complete list of everything you can think of that you might need or want for your enterprise. Do it quickly without really worrying how important each of the things is. You want to build a long list.

Next, work down your list and highlight which are wants and which are needs. You might use two different coloured highlighters for this, or simply underline one in black and one blue.

Lastly, prioritise both. Number in order of importance your top ten wants and your top ten needs. Now you have a good starting point from which to move on.

The real social entrepreneur will look for mutually beneficial relationships that reduce costs and increase customer exposure. Remember that whatever your enterprise is going to do, it has to be different to what is already out there. The best ways to be different are those that save money and reduce the risk of failure.

> **What works**
>
> Before you write your business plan, make sure you've looked beyond the obvious way of doing things. Be creative, innovative, lateral and even cheeky. People can always say no, but often they'll say yes if you suggest something that will work for them too.

Measuring social return on investment

Many social enterprises cannot survive solely on trading profits. That's because their social aim may mean they choose to operate in a way that is less profitable than their purely for-profit rivals. For example, a café that provides employment and training for people with learning disabilities will have higher staff costs than one that simply sells coffee and cakes.

The social return on investment (SROI) is the wider costs savings the social enterprise delivers. Those savings are usually made by the Government who without the social enterprise would be spending more on supporting the people in question. For example:

→ A cafe providing work for people with additional needs is saving the cost of alternative, less productive day-care.
→ An organisation that trains ex-offenders and helps them get jobs makes them less likely to re-offend. This saves the criminal justice system money.
→ An organisation that works with young people and advises on contraception reduces teenage pregnancy rates. This creates savings for the health service.

The challenge is that SROI can only be estimated, never proved. If the teenagers you work with do not get pregnant, or the ex-offender does not commit more crime, is it because of your work with them or because it would not have happened anyway? SROI is not a precise science. Statistics will exist that show the incidence of say teenage pregnancy and re-offending. If your client group delivers different proportions, you can claim the difference as your SROI.

People calculate SROI for two reasons:

➡ to put a financial value on the impact of what has been achieved, or;
➡ to estimate the financial value of what is planned.

The former is most commonly used to demonstrate to a funder the return on investment that has been achieved. This enables funders to see that their investment has made a measurable difference. That makes it easier to justify continuing the project.

The latter is used to support funding bids. It strengthens your case if, for example, you can show that by giving you £50 000 you can save your funder £150 000. This is important if you are bidding competitively for funds or applying for a grant.

How to measure SROI

The experts will tell you that there's a whole science to SROI calculations. In fact if SROI is really important to what you're doing or planning, you might find it helpful to talk to one of the many specialist consultancies working in this area.

Here are some pointers to get you started. Remember that the calculation needs to be a compromise between what your common sense tells you and what exhaustive statistical research suggests. Imagine you are providing exercise and fitness sessions for older people; consider these questions and decide how each point translates in your situation:

Question	Example
Community of interest – who are the people you work with and what defines their needs in the eyes of funders?	*'We work with older people helping them remain active and live independently.'*
Making a difference – what is it that you do that changes attitudes, behaviours, aspirations and abilities?	*'Our fitness instructors visit them at home, assessing their need, showing them exercises and lending equipment.'*
What happens if you do nothing? – in other words, what would this group do if you were not engaging them in some way?	*'These people become less mobile, suffer more from aches and pains and sometimes become lonely and depressed.'*
What's the potential public cost of doing nothing? – either look for published statistics or if you can, gain actual figures from agencies working in your area.	*'Our local university conducted a trial that suggested that on average, our weekly visits give clients on average three additional years of independent living.'*
What are the additional benefits of what you do? – although you set out to change one thing, others might also improve. What are they and what's their value?	*'Residential care for three years could cost a Local Authority £9000. Plus we reduce Health Centre workload and probably save prescription drugs too.'*
How does the money you're asking for relate to the money you think you'll save? This ratio is the SROI.	*'We charge £25 per client per week, so for three years, we charge £3900. If funded, the net saving is £5100 per client.'*

When working out SROI it is important that you:

→ **Involve** the people you expect will see savings and/or fund you in doing the calculation. If they work out the sums, they will have more faith in them.
→ **Include** the most important savings and avoid the temptation to make claims that others will consider too bold.
→ **Appreciate** the full breadth of the impact you might have and don't simply focus on the first thing you think of.
→ **Share** all of your findings, even if some contradict the argument you are trying to make. Total transparency will win you friends.
→ **Benchmark** your calculations against what actually happens with your project and others.
→ **Include** anecdotal evidence and client case studies to make it real.

Return on commercial investment

SROI was developed primarily as a tool to help charities and social enterprises show the financial impact of their work. Today however, you can apply the same methodology to demonstrate the return on investment a commercial sponsor might gain.

This is important because we are all becoming far more interested in the ethical, environmental and economic impact of the companies we deal with. For the corporate business world, being good at what you do is no longer enough. You have to be good without detriment to others. For example:

→ Nestle and Starbucks now sell Fair Trade products, evidence that they are doing more to support the farmers who grow the products they sell.

→ Highland Spring bottled water is taken from natural springs beneath Soil Association organically managed farmland. The company also sponsors community events near its bottling plant. It is recognised by many as an ethical company.

→ Nissan are investing more than £400m in a new UK plant that will produce 50 000 electric cars a year.

Faber Castel are a large and diverse international company. One of their core products is pencils. They produce literally millions of them a year.

In the 1980s, long before most companies thought about social and environmental impact, Faber Castel started planting trees in Brazil. They planted tracts of land most had thought could not be cultivated and so created new areas of forest.

Now they have their own supply of timber for pencils and replace each tree they cut down. They also use water based paints on their pencils. These are better for the environment and make their pencils safer to chew than unpainted pencils.

These factors contribute to their popularity, their profitability and their environmental impact.

As a social entrepreneur, you can help businesses big and small improve their customer appeal in a number of ways. They can provide you with materials, space and expertise. They can provide work experience and employment for people you are helping get their lives back on track. When all else is equal, most customers will choose to do business with the organisation they feel cares most about them, about their community and about their impact on the environment.

You can follow the same SROI track when planning how to encourage the business community to support your social enterprise. Take a second look at those SROI questions and see how they translate benefits a business might fund. If you remember the example given related to a project that helps keep older people active, mobile and living independently:

➤ A local gym might provide equipment and off-peak classes for your clients.
➤ A local coach company might sponsor you and sell day excursions to your clients.
➤ A provider of mobility scooters might sponsor you to show that they care about your mobility and don't simply want to sell you a scooter.

What works

The best social entrepreneurs are those who define each separate group for whom they add value, define that value and convert it into income. Social enterprise can and should involve a wider community than its customers and beneficiaries.

Some headings to help you get it right first time

So now you should be ready to put pen to paper and start to write your business plan. You have a vision, mission and values. You've considered what it is you want to do, why and who will benefit. You have also looked at how different groups will benefit in different ways from what you do. Now use these headings and write your plan as clearly and concisely as you can.

Title and strapline

You might be planning a new business or simply a new venture within an existing organisation. Give the plan a title that makes it clear which this is. Add a strapline that captures the very essence of your vision and mission.

EG: Fit Folk CIC – Keeping folk active longer

Executive summary

In four short paragraphs summarise exactly:

→ What you are going to do.
→ Where you are going to do it.
→ Why it is needed and why you're well placed to meet that need.
→ How you're going to make it financially viable.

EG: Fit Folk CIC would include that they provide fitness instructors to visit older people to improve their mobility and independence funded by a mix of client fees and public sector grant based on the SROI.

Vision/Mission/Values

List the phrases you have already developed (in Chapter 6) that explain:

→ The difference you want to make.
→ How you are going to do it.
→ What values will define and differentiate you from others.

EG: Fit Folk CIC would include their vision for fitness in extreme old age and their mission to keep people active for longer. Their values would define their motivation for doing this work, perhaps having witnessed needless physical decline.

Structure and governance

Structures are explored in the next chapter. You need to say here:

→ How you will be constituted and why that choice.
→ Who will hold you accountable – for example, non exec Directors, Trustees or perhaps an advisory group.
→ Briefly, how this will be achieved – i.e. quarterly Board meetings.

Context

Here you need to set the scene for what you plan to do:

→ What are the dimensions, boundaries and capacity of your marketplace?
→ What are the political, environmental, economic, social and technological issues that shape your marketplace and create your opportunity?
→ What is changing to create your opportunity and will demand change over time?

EG: Fit Folk CIC might refer here to research findings that quantify the benefits of what they do. This will help later in calculating SROI.

Activities

Now you need to define the things you are going to be doing. Some may be things you get paid for and others things fund with the money you earn. Focus just on the most important or significant and list:

→ What products or services you will provide and to whom?
→ Where are the linkages between these and what else happens?
→ What volume of activity will take place and how will it grow?

EG: Fit Folk CIC might list the types of fitness therapy they will deliver and map this against other local provision to show where they fit.

Customers

You may have a number of customer groups, each with different needs and expectations. Show you understand that by listing them, together with what they're going to buy. This can get complicated, so here's a table to prompt you. It's based on the earlier example of Fit Folk CIC:

Customer Group	Buys
Older people – your clients	Subsidised fitness instruction
Friends and relatives of the above	Gift vouchers for fitness sessions
Social services provide a grant	Deferment of expensive, intensive care

Customer Group	Buys
Local businesses provide modest sponsorship	Publicity for the businesses Product/service introduction to clients
Local grant makers	Grants that are extended by match funding from your other customers

Resources

What do you need to deliver these activities? Remember the earlier point about focusing on the things you need. If there are things you want but can acquire, this is where you explain how. Remember to include:

→ People you might hire or recruit as associates or sub-contractors.
→ Premises you might need and where else you will be operating.
→ Equipment you need, its cost and capacity.
→ Materials and where you will source them.

> *EG: Fit Folk CIC could not only list the people, vehicles and equipment they need but compare the cost to those of running a specialist gym and bringing clients in. It's good to consider options and justify choice.*

Marketing

Key to your success will be your ability to attract customers and generate revenue. To do this you might consider:

➥ Brand – how you package your offer in a way that is visible and memorable.

➥ Position – where you fit in the marketplace (quality/price/complexity).

➥ Promotion – how you are going to build awareness and recruit customers.

EG: Fit Folk CIC could explain how it will gain referrals from doctors and social workers, as well as advertise to reach the older people themselves.

Investment

How much money are you going to need, where will you find it and over what period you will pay it back? Remember that (depending on the legal structure you adopt) as a social enterprise you can:

➥ apply for grants from a number of sources;

➥ issue shares and give dividends to your shareholders;

➥ borrow money from banks and specialist lenders;

➥ attract investment or donation from individuals and organisations;

➥ sometimes entitle your investors to tax concessions.

Cash flow and profitability

Finally you need a simple cash flow forecast for your enterprise. It's usually good to produce two versions, one bold and one cautious. In the less bold version, you can show the impact of business taking off more slowly than planned and people delaying payment. These are the two main problems new enterprises encounter. Your cash flow needs to be set out like this:

	Month 1	Month 2	Month 3 etc	Total
Opening bank balance				
Income – one line per activity				
Total income				
Variable costs – link to sales				
Costs – one line per type				
Total costs– money spent				
Closing bank balance				

When putting together cash flow projections people often forget to include:

→ employment costs such as national insurance which add around 11% to your wage bill;
→ VAT which you may or may not register for, charge and reclaim. It affects cash flow significantly;
→ easy to overlook costs such as business rates, insurance and training.

EG: Fit Folk CIC would want to show in particular the balance between client income and contract funding. There might also be start-up grant funding and loans to repay, and lastly, donations of vehicle lease and fitness equipment. It is good to show that you have been frugal.

In summary

🐣 Make your business plan simple, short and specific.

🐣 Plan to invest in the things you need and to acquire, share or wait for the things you want.

🐣 Consider SROI and help funders recognise the full value of what you do.

🐣 Apply the principles of SROI to help you win support from businesses too.

🐣 When you write your business plan, use the suggested headings (or similar) to summarise the project. Create appendices so that detail, for example statistics and market analysis, can be easily found.

Find out more

The SROI network   sroi-uk.org

SROI calculator   socialevaluator.eu

Social Enterprise Coalition   socialenterprise.org.uk/pages/
   'business support tools'   tools

8

What You Need to Know about Structure and Governance

'It is our choices ... that show what we truly are, far more than our abilities'.

J K Rowling, *Harry Potter and The Chamber of Secrets*, 1999

Points to consider

O nce you have started to write your business plan, it is time to consider legal structure. Social entrepreneurs can be found working within all types of organisations. Your choice of organisational structure will be defined by your:

→ **Starting point** – are you creating a totally new organisation or are you creating a new venture within an existing one? Perhaps your project is a partnership or collaboration between two or more existing organisations? Your first consideration has to be where you are right now.

→ **Vision and goal** – how big do you see your enterprise growing? Where will it operate? You need to choose a structure that will suit what the organisation will become, not what it is right now. Changing structures can be costly and time consuming. You want a structure you can grow into, not one you grow out of.

→ **Turnover and life expectancy** – if your project is more about volunteer activity than income you might be fine as you are. Many very successful projects remain informal community groups, perhaps with a basic constitution and bank account. Equally, if your focus is a single festival or other event, then providing you keep good records, it might not be worth setting up a new organisation.

→ **Exposure to risk** – many self-employed people and partnerships incorporate (become limited companies) to separate personal assets from their business ones. This means that should their business fail, personal assets are normally protected. As a social entrepreneur, you have an added incentive to legally separate your finances from those of your enterprise. If you are being funded in any way to make a difference, you need to be able to show clearly how you have accounted for your income and expenditure.

Almost any entrepreneur starting out on a new venture would consider these questions. Every organisation, project or campaign has a starting point, vision and needs to manage risk. As a social entrepreneur, you have even more things to consider. For example, you will have a vision for people and planet as well as profit.

This means you have more to consider and perhaps a wider choice of structures to select from. Here are some questions you might ask yourself and those working with you.

- ➡ **Ownership** – who is going to own your enterprise? Will it be owned by its employees, or perhaps by community shareholders clubbing together to buy a community asset such as a pub. You might also want to own a share of the enterprise yourself and receive income from it. Or perhaps an existing organisation, such as a charity, will own what you hope will become a trading division. Finally you might want to attract investors. There's a lot to think about.
- ➡ **Governance** – do you want to involve key stakeholders and investors in setting direction and measuring performance? Do you want this to be a formal arrangement, such as a Board of Directors or Trustees, or simply an advisory group? Remember that the more responsibility you give, the greater the commitment.
- ➡ **Control** – entrepreneurial people often prefer to retain control of the organisations they start. If you want overall control, you'll probably opt to create a limited company rather than a charity. Conversely, if you want to set up an organisation that others will manage, you might choose to set up a charity with Trustees who like you, volunteer their time to steer the organisation.
- ➡ **Income** – the principle of social enterprise is to generate profits that can be wholly or partly used to meet a

recognised social or environmental need. As you know from the previous chapter, few social enterprises make all of their money from straightforward trade. Most rely on income from grants, subsidies or by providing more effective (and often lower cost) services on behalf of public sector agencies.

Choosing the right structure

As you can see, choosing the right structure is not as simple as it might first appear. It's always good to seek professional advice before taking the plunge. Many ask their accountant or a solicitor. Both can usually help, providing you choose a professional with social enterprise experience.

What works

When looking for professional advisers ask other entrepreneurs you respect for recommendations. The best people are almost always found in this way.

It really is important to consider your own position and personal aims when choosing which legal structure to adopt. It is also worth remembering that people with the skills to start an organisation often lack the focus to manage and grow them in the long term.

In other words, include your own exit strategy in your thinking and try to avoid setting up an organisation in such a way as to make it dependant on you. Equally, make sure you retain the control you feel you need. You don't want to fall victim to a boardroom coup!

Structures to choose from

Having thought about what you want to achieve, you now have to consider each of the possible legal structures for your organisation or project. Most commonly found are charities, limited liability companies and community interest companies. Before looking at each of these in detail, here's a list of the ten different legal structures you might encounter.

Unincorporated Association

A common starting point for many initiatives, an Unincorporated Association costs nothing to set up and is not registered or regulated by any national organisation. They are usually started by groups of like minded individuals who commit to a common cause. For example, a group of neighbours decide to work together to raise money to tidy up their neighbourhood and organise some community events.

> **Geldeston Community Composting Group** is a village group that collects local garden and kitchen waste for composting. It earns money from selling compost to gardeners and claims recycling credits for waste that would otherwise have gone to landfill. The group won a grant to buy a trailer with which volunteers collect waste.

Unincorporated Associations usually have (or quickly create):

- a management committee and democratic decision making;
- a simple written constitution;
- a bank account;

They usually do not:

→ have employees, being entirely volunteer run;
→ own property (unless held separately in a simple legal Trust);
→ grow very large before converting to a more formal, legal structure.

They can apply for grants. Some funders, for example Community Foundations, make a point of supporting these small groups because they are often community led and grow into significant charities and social enterprises if helped in the early days.

Members of the association are potentially personally liable for any leases or agreements they sign on behalf of the group. It is usually when the stakes get higher that unincorporated associations decide to become limited companies or register as a charity.

They can also trade and frequently do, although usually on a small modest scale.

What works

Setting up an **Unincorporated Association** is a good way to start a community based social enterprise. Once you have won local commitment and proved the concept you will probably want to convert it into something more formal.

Trusts

A Trust is a legal vehicle which enables people to hold assets on behalf of others. Those who hold the asset are called

Trustees. The terms of the Trust, i.e. the conditions it imposes on the Trustees, dictate how that asset should be used.

It is not a legally incorporated organisation, nor does it distribute profits. It is created with a set of legally binding, governing rules which are applied by the Trustees. Charities often hold assets in Trust and the Trustees of the charity also act as Trustees of the Trust.

You will most commonly encounter:

Development Trusts – usually hold community buildings and other assets gifted to a community by Local Government. They are community owned and managed and often established to regenerate a neighbourhood. They provide a hub within and from which other community organisations can work. Transferring public buildings and spaces into community ownership in this way:

➡ prevents them from being sold and lost to the community;
➡ makes it more appealing for local people to volunteer to run services from them, as ownership now sits with the community;

It enables the former owners, often Local Government, to free themselves of:

Community Land Trusts – are similar to Development Trusts except that their focus is almost always on the property itself. Whereas a Development Trust is focused on regeneration activities as part of which it holds assets, a Community Land Trust may acquire land and buildings which it lets, or operates shared ownership schemes to provide affordable housing.

Householders can buy their home bit by bit, renting the remainder until they own their home outright.

Social enterprises acquiring land and buildings, for example building a replacement for a community hospital and health centre, often create a Community Land Trust to hold the assets on their behalf. This prevents the property from ever being sold, protecting the operating social enterprise.

Woodthorpe Development Trust grew out of a community initiative on a run down estate in Sheffield. Local residents felt their community was being ignored by support agencies and decided to do something themselves. It is both a company limited by guarantee and a registered charity, running a number of community services to generate 60% of its income (the balance coming from grants). Profits are reinvested in the community it serves. The organisation holds a number of community buildings in Trust and employs 30 people.

Woodthorpe Development Trust:

- is set up as a Development Trust;
- holds its community buildings in a Community Land Trust;
- trades as a 'company limited by guarantee.'

Trusts usually:

⟶ hold assets in perpetuity for community use;
⟶ are operated by Trustees who may also run a related trading company;
⟶ manage those assets for the benefit of their community.

They usually do not:

⟶ distribute profits outside the communities they serve;

➤ rely solely on grant income, but make money too;

➤ exist in isolation, but more usually are a legal structure within a charity or limited company;

They can acquire community assets and are often encouraged to do so. In many cases they take over publicly run facilities that are at risk of closure.

What works

Setting up a **Trust** enables a community to take over and hold buildings and land in a way that retains assets in community ownership for community benefit.

Limited Company

A limited company is a legal entity in its own right (a sole trader or a partnership is a trading identity of the proprietor or partners). This means the company's finances are completely separate from those of its shareholders or Directors.

Shareholder liability is limited to the value of their shares. Shares capital is the money invested in the company. Profits can be distributed to shareholders as dividends. If the company fails, shareholders lose their share capital.

If the company grows it can become a 'public limited company' and have its shares traded on the stock market. Until that happens though, it remains a private limited company, with shares bought and sold privately.

For the social entrepreneur, setting up a limited company is a good way to separate the business from their personal affairs.

All limited companies:

➡ Have a memorandum of understanding and articles of association (Memo and Arts). These are effectively the constitution of the business and define some of the rules by which the company is governed.
➡ Are owned by their shareholders, (providing the company is limited by shares) who appoint the Directors.
➡ Each share normally carries one vote but voting rights may depend on the class of share, so a majority shareholder has a majority vote.

When a limited company is set up, its 'memo & arts' will usually be adapted from a standard model document to meet the specific needs of the venture. For example, you can write into your 'memo & arts' the way in which you wish your profits to be distributed and your assets protected for the cause you are committed to supporting.

Limited companies can:

➡ appoint non executive Directors who help the Directors working in the business with strategy and direction;
➡ set up subsidiary companies, wholly owned or shared with others;
➡ own property;
➡ open their own bank account;
➡ borrow money, although banks usually ask Directors to personally guarantee the loan;

Few grant makers will make awards to limited companies. This is because the structure is not easily associated with organisations with a strong social or environmental purpose. Even if you have adapted your memo & arts to commit the business to your cause, that commitment is not transparent and so open to abuse.

Finally, limited companies can also be limited by guarantee rather than share. In this instance there are no issued shares, but a number of members who each guarantee the debts of the business. That guarantee is usually limited to £1.00 per member.

The members effectively act as shareholders, appointing Directors who then run the business. Because there are no shares, no profits can be distributed. Instead they remain within the company and can be applied to further the cause for which the organisation was established.

Companies limited by guarantee (rather than share) can apply for grants because the funder can see clearly that profits will be re-invested and not distributed to private shareholders.

Trade associations, membership organisations and many community organisations structure themselves as a company limited by guarantee.

> **! What works**
>
> Many trading subsidiaries of charities are set up as 'companies limited by guarantee'. The company will then gift its profits back to the parent charity. This protects the parent charity from undue financial risk and keeps its trading activities clearly distinct from its core activities and fundraising.

Community Interest Companies (CIC)

A CIC is a limited company that comes with some specific additions to its 'memo & arts' that make clear the company's social purpose in a widely accepted way. Implicit from the name, every CIC has to have and define its 'community of interest'. That is the group of people for whose benefit the organisation is being established. CICs were introduced in the UK in 2005.

At least 65% of a CIC's distributable profits must be used to benefit that community of interest, with the remaining 35% available for distribution to shareholders as dividends, subject to the dividend cap. This means that investors can receive a return on their investment. However, share value appreciation is capped and assets owned by the CIC are 'locked' and cannot be sold. You have to nominate another CIC or charity to receive any residual assets should your CIC be wound up.

Where a CIC is limited by guarantee there are no shares and so all profits are retained within the business.

To register as a CIC the company has to pass a 'Community Interest Test', proving in its application that it is indeed being set up with social or environmental good as its prime purpose. Each year, your annual return to Companies House has to be accompanied by a written statement confirming you remain focused on serving your 'community of interest'. The test is described by Companies House as: 'whether a reasonable person might consider that the company's activities are being carried on for the benefit of the community'. There is a simple form you return each year on which you describe how your company meets this requirement. If those reading it are not sure, they will usually ask for clarification.

In all other respects, a CIC is a limited company. It can be limited by share or guarantee and can also become a public limited company.

Benefits of establishing a social enterprise as a CIC include:

➡ A binding commitment to benefit your community of interest more than your shareholders.

➡ The ability to issue shares and pay modest dividends. In reality this means that investors do not see huge gains, but neither do they lose out.

➡ The opportunity, in some circumstances for investors to gain tax relief on their investment in recognition of its speculative nature (e.g. Enterprise Investment Scheme in the UK).

➡ The ability to pay both executive and non–executive Directors with greater ease than if you registered as a charity.

➡ Wide recognition by grant makers who may fund CICs but will not accept applications from other forms of Limited Company.

What works

Creating a CIC limited by share enables you to both attract investors and apply for grants. It blends the transparency of purpose of a charity with the commercial flexibility of a limited company.

Get it right first time

Because CICs are still relatively new, they are less widely understood amongst professional advisers (unless they specialise in social enterprise). Providing you know what it is you want to do, it is not difficult to set up a CIC. Here are some specific tips to help you get it right first time:

➡ Your CIC cannot share the name of any other limited company registered with Companies House. Search the register online to check what's already taken. This is free of charge and called 'Webcheck'.

→ CIC36 is the form on which you define your 'community of interest'. It is easy to understand and simple to fill in. Do this yourself.

→ CIC34 is the form you download and fill in to submit with your annual return. Take a look before your accountant worries you about it.

→ Your application form will be returned to you if:

- it is incorrectly filled in;
- the name you have chosen is not available;
- your CIC36 is not clear enough in explaining what you are going to do.

→ It is often worthwhile finding a social enterprise business adviser to help you, as well as your accountant. Most applications will benefit from the expertise of both, although with a little time and effort you should be capable of completing the application yourself.

Industrial and Provident Society (IPS)

These are legally constituted organisations that conduct industry, business or trade, either as a cooperative for the benefit of their members, or for the benefit of a wider community.

An IPS has share capital, with share value dictated by current business performance. In a cooperative, the shares are owned by the members, who may also share the profits as dividends although more usually profits are re-invested.

When not a cooperative, but for a wider community benefit, there is usually a specific reason why this structure has been adopted rather than a limited company. For example, a credit union or other social lender will raise investment from its shareholders and lend to people denied access to credit from banks. The IPS structure provides a convenient and often tax efficient vehicle for this.

Oxford Bread Group is a cooperative set up to make tasty, healthy, ecologically-sound bread available to all who want it. The cooperative makes and distributes artisan bread to its members. New members are asked to join for at least three months, paying £30 which entitles them to 12 loaves of bread. Bread is baked centrally and distributed via a network of local collection hubs. The organisation exists solely for the benefit of its members.

Industrial and Provident Societies usually have:

→ a membership democracy where each member has an equal vote;
→ a written constitution or set of rules that conform to a standard;
→ status as an 'unregistered charity' if not a cooperative.

Foundation East is a social lender created to provide loans to people wanting to start or grow a business, but unable to meet the lending criteria of the High Street banks. They recruit shareholders who can derive tax benefits from investing in the organisation. A team of loan advisers help applicants prepare their funding pitch and support them if they are successful.

They are most usually set up:

→ to meet the needs of a group of people with a common interest;

➡ by a workers cooperative seeking a collective organisational structure;

➡ as a vehicle for community fund raising, for example to buy a community building;

➡ as a social lender, usually either a credit union or 'credit development funding initiative';

Because they are created 'not for profit' they can often apply for grants. They also trade and so are true social enterprises.

Market Overton Village Shop – When their village shop owner announced they were going to close up, locals clubbed together and raised more than £50000 in 16 weeks to take the business over and run it themselves.

They did it by setting up an IPS and inviting their neighbours to become shareholders. Not only was this a good way to raise the investment needed, it created a real sense of ownership with shareholders eager to support the shop they helped to buy and collectively own.

Get it right first time

If you are setting up an IPS to act as a vehicle for raising funds for a community project, there are also arguments for setting up as a CIC. You need to take expert advice and be sure you understand the pros and cons of both options before deciding. It is also worth talking to community groups that have already done it because they can talk you through how they made their decision and how with hindsight, they might have acted differently.

Charity Incorporated Organisation (CIO)

This new structure has been subject of lengthy consultation and is expected to come into existence during 2011. Charities exploring social enterprise may consider registering as a CIO as an alternative to creating a wholly owned trading subsidiary.

It is also expected to provide a convenient middle ground for charities that currently operate both as a registered charity and company limited by guarantee. Currently, dual registered charities have to provide two sets of accounts, each requiring different levels and styles of reporting.

Charities

Registered charities traditionally received and made grants, created endowments from which grants are made, and met social and environmental needs through direct activity. Increasingly they are boosting their income from fundraising by trading. For example, many operate charity shops and sell services to subsidise those they provide for free to those in need.

It is unlikely that as a social entrepreneur, you would choose the charity structure for your new organisation. However, if you are already working within an existing charity, you will find that your charity's governing documents, together with current tax regulations will define the extent to which you can generate income from social enterprise activity.

 What works

Because charities in the UK enjoy tax concessions, so too are they limited in the extent to which they can trade. If

> you're starting from within an existing charity, always discuss your plans with the organisation's tax advisers first.

Get it right first time

Setting up a charity can be quite easy. However, if you plan to trade in any significant way you might find the structure of a registered charity too restrictive. As stated earlier, many charities also set up trading companies. You might want to avoid having to produce two sets of accounts and follow two sets of governance regulations.

In summary

- Your choice of legal structure should be based on your medium term goal, not your immediate need.
- The structure you choose must meet you own needs as well as funder expectations.
- Always take professional advice and ask around to find the right adviser.
- Try not to compromise your vision to fit with a recommended organisational structure. Try to find the right structure for what you want to do.

Find out more

Social Enterprise London – free downloads
sel.org.uk/publications

Community Foundations
communityfoundations.org.uk

Woodthorpe Development Trust
woodthorpedt.co.uk

Community Land Trusts	communitylandtrusts.org.uk
Development Trusts Association	dta.org.uk
CIC Regulator	cicregulator.gov.uk
CIC Association	cicassociation.org.uk
Companies House	companieshouse.gov.uk
Cooperatives UK	cooperatives-uk.coop
Financial Services Authority (IPS)	http://tinyurl.com/2fknubv
Oxford Bread Group	oxfordlocalbread.org
Foundation East	foundationeast.org
UK Charity Commission	charitycommission.gov.uk

9

Finding the Funding

'Money is better than poverty, if only for financial reasons.'

Woody Allen, *Without Feathers*, 1976

Capital and cashflow – why they're different

ash is the lifeblood of every business. If you or your enterprise have too little, fainting and collapse will follow. You will also soon bleed to death if a damaged artery is not quickly repaired, so too will a business quickly die if it haemorrhages money without rapid remedial treatment.

There are two kinds of money in any organisation. Capital is the money invested in buying the things you need to operate; premises, vehicles, equipment, etc. Cash is the money that customers give you which you then spend on materials and running costs such as labour, rent and expenses. To start or grow any organisation, you need both.

When your focus is on delivering social or environmental change, the financial management of your organisation can be confusing. But unless you get the finances right, nothing else will happen. As the previous chapter explains, the confusion can be compounded by the fact that you might have several different sources of income, some grant and some from trade.

An easy way to differentiate between capital and cash is this:

→ Capital flows through the business slowly.
→ Cash flows in and out of the business quickly.

Capital

To set up almost any enterprise you need capital to buy the things you need. Clearly the less capital you need, the easier it will be to find. Even if you are setting up a new venture within a public sector or large organisation, you will have to make a strong case for capital funding. That's because there will be others pitching for the same money, so the stronger your case, the better your chance of success.

When looking for capital, you need to look for:

⟶ loans that you pay back slowly over a long period;
⟶ grants that you don't have to repay at all;
⟶ investment from people who will not want their money back until you're ready to repay them.

Cash

Much to the puzzlement of even the most experienced business owner, you can be very busy with lots of sales but have no money in the bank. That's because there's inevitably a gap between your incurring costs and being paid for what those costs have produced.

When looking for working capital to finance your cash flow you need to look for:

⟶ an overdraft;
⟶ revenue grants;
⟶ customers who pay you early;
⟶ suppliers who allow you to pay late.

Example

Imagine that you run an employment project that makes and sells bird tables. You rent your premises but have to buy tools and some woodworking machines and a van. You then need to buy timber, make the tables and sell them. Three local garden centres stock your bird tables on a 'sale or return basis'.

You need capital to buy the equipment, fit out the workshops and buy the van. This you get part as a grant and part as a bank loan. You are then set up ready to start.

You next need to hire staff and recruit your trainees, for whom you receive a training allowance. You also need a stock of timber, nails and paint. You also need to run the van and make sure you are insured and pay your rent. All of these costs are covered by your working capital, although some you might cover with a long term loan or grant.

Income comes from two sources; training grants and bird table sales.

Here's what your monthly cash flow might look like:

	Month 1 Set up	Month 2 People arrive	Month 3 Make tables	Month 4 Sell tables
Grants/loan	20,000			
Training allowance		2,000	2,000	2,000
Table sales				1,000
Total Income	**20,000**	**2,000**	**2,000**	**3,000**
Set up costs	20,000			
Materials			500	500
Staff costs		2,000	2,000	2,000
Total spend	**20,000**	**2,000**	**2,500**	**2,500**
Balance	**0**	**0**	**−500**	**+500**

In this simple example, even though you sell your tables quite quickly and can see that once established, you'll make £500 per month profit, in month three you have a deficit of £500. If sales are slower picking up, or if your funder pays you late, you quickly run out of money to buy materials or pay staff.

The easiest way to bridge the gap is by having an overdraft. Or you could ask your funder to pay in advance, or your materials supplier to accept late payment. Most enterprises use a combination of all three to even out the peaks and troughs of cash flow.

What works

When planning how much working capital you'll need, always add 25% to what your calculations say you'll need. Give yourself some headroom so that small set backs don't cause you major problems.

Grants

Because as a social entrepreneur you choose to sacrifice some profit to benefit the people and the planet, your enterprise may qualify for grant funding. That's not to say you can forego the need to become financially viable. But it does mean you can often bid for capital grants to reduce your need for long term borrowing.

Your ability to apply for grants will depend on a number of factors:

→ Your **legal structure** and the extent to which this guarantees that grants received are applied solely for the benefit of your case.
→ The social or environmental **need** for what it is you're going to do and more importantly, your ability to quantify that need.

➡ How well you can show that your team have the **skills, techniques** and proven methodologies for delivering lasting change.

➡ The extent to which the grant will be levering **match funding** from other sources. Grant makers like to see their money making a big difference.

➡ What **support** you have amongst others working in the same field.

Anytown Healthcare CIC – Concerned that their local Community Hospital was uneconomically small and at risk of closure, the Hospital's League of Friends led the establishment of Anytown Healthcare CIC. The organisation was awarded a grant from the Department of Health to develop a robust business plan that would enable the hospital beds to be retained within the community, but in a form the NHS could afford to fund.

The CIC decided to set up a nursing home for which there was a local need. Contained within it would be a community hospital wing, which as part of a larger unit could operate profitably and offer the NHS a reduction in costs.

The project cost almost £3m and was funded:

- by the local NHS Trust that purchased the land for the new unit;
- by a sizeable donation made from the League of Friends' reserves;
- by a commercial loan from the NHS 'Social Enterprise Investment Fund'
- by issuing shares to local people who invested in the venture and will gain a modest return on their investment under the CIC rules.

Funding you

Social entrepreneurs emerge from a variety of places. Sometimes they need help with their living costs whilst they develop their idea into an enterprise. If you're developing an idea that will help your current employer, they may well give you paid time off to work on your plan. However, that's not always the case.

Unltd is a charitable organisation set up in 2002 to promote and support entrepreneurship.

They can sometimes fund your living expenses as well as project costs with a 'Level 2' Award of up to £15 000. To qualify you must have been trading for at least a year, have set up a legally constituted organisation and be generating at least some income to show that your project is viable.

Funding around the world

Wherever you are in the world, and wherever you plan to work as a social entrepreneur, there are organisations able to offer you help, advice and sometimes funding. You can identify possible funders by:

- ➡ looking to see who major global donors such as the Bill & Melinda Gates Foundation have supported in your region, then approaching them;
- ➡ exploring the Overseas Development Departments of wealthy counties with strong trading or heritage links to your country;
- ➡ contacting international companies who from your research have budgets for Corporate Social Responsibility.
- ➡ networking with other local social entrepreneurs to find out where they found support.

Funding your project

As well as Unltd who will fund you before you have established any legal structure, there are a number of other places you can look for grant funding. These will include:

Who	How
Local Councils	Download and read their economic strategy and see if and how your project fits with what they want to see.
Government	Some Government departments (e.g. Dept of Health) have established grant and loan funds to help their employees create social enterprises. Check online.
Community Foundations	These are locally based and each has a different range of grant opportunities. Find your local Foundation and ask their grants officer for advice.
Grant Making Trusts	A number of Trusts will accept applications from social enterprises. A number of UK Trusts are listed below to get you started.
Companies	Both major national companies and small local businesses may well support your social enterprise. Ask around and see what you can discover.

Example

Telecoms company O2 launched 'Think Big', a £5m programme in 2010 that provides grants of £300 to young people aged 13–25 to fund their community development ideas. Some will apply through existing community organisations and some will be funded direct.

Grant-making Trusts

There are literally thousands of grant-making Trusts, each with its own criteria for assessing bids. Most focus on helping charities and community groups, but some will help social enterprises. To qualify, your legal structure and constitution will have to match what they will support. To help you make a start, here are some you can check out.

→ Calouste Gulbenkian Foundation
→ Esmee Fairbairn Foundation
→ LankellyChase Foundation
→ The Baring Foundation
→ The Barrow Cadbury Trust
→ The Big Lottery Fund
→ The Henry Smith Charity
→ The Joseph Rowntree Charitable Trust
→ The Tudor Trust

What works

Most grant making Trusts welcome telephone enquiries. If their website suggests they might be able to help you, ring and ask before spending a lot of time making an application. This saves time for both you and them!

If you cannot find any grants

Grants can enable you to get off the ground faster but it's not the end of the world if you find it impossible to get grant funding to help you start. In the absence of grants, you simply have to be more entrepreneurial. Here are a few ways other entrepreneurs have got started with very little investment:

→ Significant customers, particularly those in the public sector, might well be willing to pay you in advance. This is more likely if they expect to work with you for a year or so.
→ Suppliers can give you extended credit. This also goes for your landlord if you need premises. Just make sure you ask first, rather than simply stall payment.
→ Approach a local successful entrepreneur and excite them with your plan. They might lend you some money to get started and mentor you until you have repaid the loan. If you get them really passionate about your venture, they might leave their cash in and help you grow your organisation.

Banks and mainstream lenders

Banks will lend money to anyone who meets their criteria for a loan. There are many banks to choose from as well as the big names on the High Street. Remember that you can have a working relationship with more than one bank. For example, you might have a loan from one to cover capital purchases and do your day to day banking with another with whom you may also have an overdraft facility.

In fact choosing banks to work with can be daunting. Most will offer very similar services although their attitudes to lending could be quite different. Make sure you:

→ talk to more than one before choosing which one to work with;
→ ask around for recommendations from other social entrepreneurs;
→ don't assume that the bank you use for your private finances will also be the best choice for your enterprise.

What banks look for

You will know from your business plan what you need to borrow to get your social enterprise started. You also will have produced a cash flow forecast and remembered to err on the side of caution and be seeking an overdraft limit that gives you breathing space. But what is your bank looking for? Well in short, they want you to represent a low risk and to clearly be capable of repaying the loan.

CAMPARI is a useful acronym that banks often use as part of their decision making. It will help you to use this too as you prepare your proposal.

Character – Do you have integrity, a clean personal credit history and a strong commitment to your project?

→ Do gather references that support your reputation.
→ Do not give the impression that your passion is clouding your judgement.

Ability – Do you know what you are talking about and have both relevant experience and the right people working with you? Are you looking for money to realise a plan or to respond to a crisis you should have foreseen?

➺ Do use your CV and career successes to illustrate your abilities.
➺ Do not suggest that you know better than others in your field.

Margin – Does the deal look good for the bank as well as for you? Are you being realistic about your trading margins? Will you be profitable throughout the loan period?

➺ Do set out to make profits, even if you choose to reinvest them in the project.
➺ Do not build your business case around continued grant or public funding.

Purpose – What do you need the money for? Is it for something constructive or to get you out of a tight corner?

➺ Do make sure you explain exactly what you plan to do with the investment;
➺ Do not even hint that it's needed because you've made an earlier mistake.

Amount – Are you being realistic in what you are asking for? Are you being overambitious? Where else are you getting investment from?

➺ Do provide realistic cash flow forecasts.
➺ Do not say that success is pre-ordained and to be taken as read.

Repayment – How manageable are the proposed repayments? What will your project look like in the later years? Is there a risk that the loan debt will outline the project?

➡ Do show both the changing need and your planned growth beyond the life of the loan.
➡ Do not show monthly forecasts beyond three years because they'll be based on guess work. Most people expect quarterly figures after year three.

Insurance – What guarantees can you give the bank to reduce their risk? Are there assets over which they can take a legal charge? Lastly, what happens if you die?

➡ Do insure the lives of key people so that the loan is covered.
➡ Do not say that because it's not for profit the bank should take the risk.

Consider each of these points, both from your own perspective and your bank manager's. Put yourself in his shoes and even get someone whose opinion you trust to read your business plan and funding proposal and give you objective feedback.

 What works
Not all bank managers understand social enterprise. Emphasise how you will make money and your organisation sustainable.

Specialist lenders and why they're different

There are a number of specialist lenders that social entrepreneurs can approach. These tend to be more in tune with the concept of social enterprise and prepared to make at least some concessions to your social or environmental purpose. That's not to say they won't be rigorous in their assessment of the risk, but at least they will understand your motivation.

There are a number of different kinds of lender you can consider:

Specialist banks

Banks with a special interest in social enterprise lending include:

→ **Triodos Bank** – a full service bank offering services to individuals, investors and borrowers. It focuses on meeting the banking needs of people and organisations wishing to encourage corporate social responsibility and a sustainable society.
→ **Charity Bank** – despite its name, this bank also lends to some forms of social enterprise, particularly Community Interest Companies and Industrial and Provident Societies.
→ **Cooperative Bank** – is unique in that as a cooperative that belongs to its members it is itself a social enterprise. Like the other two examples, it provides a wide range of banking services.

Big Issue Invest

Part of the same group of companies as the 'Big Issue' magazine, Big Issue Invest is an investment fund that lends money to social enterprises. For its investors, it is an alternative private equity vehicle that invests solely in social enterprises and trading arms of charities. Loans range between £50 000 and £250 000, with those seeking larger investments dealt with in partnership with other social finance institutions.

Community Development Finance Institutions (CDFI)

CDFIs traditionally provide loans to people who face barriers to accessing finance. For example, they may lend to individuals with a poor credit history or little collateral, or provide business loans to entrepreneurs with little business experience. There are both national and local CDFIs, each with its own lending criteria and objectives.

CDFIs tend to make far smaller loans than, say Big Issue Invest and to focus on people creating enterprises to overcome some disadvantage. Some of these will be social enterprises.

They will typically lend money to provide:

→ working capital;
→ bridging finance;
→ equipment purchase.

Because CDFIs are lenders of last resort, they often charge higher interest rates than mainstream lenders. However, the rates they charge are considerably lower than the alternative sources of finance for people denied credit elsewhere.

Investors – your unique opportunity

Some legal structures, specifically CICs limited by share and Industrial and Provident Societies, enable you to recruit investors. Organisations such as Big Issue Invest can take an equity stake in a growing social enterprise, enabling their own investors, as well as your own, to profit from the success that investment funds.

More commonly, shares are issued so that community members can literally own a stake in a community enterprise. Community shops and pubs are increasingly passing into community ownership when they become uneconomically viable as 'for profit' concerns.

Enabling local residents to become shareholders in a community resource is important for a number of reasons:

→ It places ownership firmly within the community and because of the way such organisations are usually structured, the asset cannot be sold on for, say, re-development as housing.
→ Because local residents are co-owners they are far more likely to patronise the business. This helps to make it financially more viable than it would otherwise have been.
→ Shareholders also become involved as volunteers, getting 'hands on' with the business they own with their neighbours. This enables a village shop, for example, to open for longer hours without the labour costs that might render longer hours uneconomic.

The Burrow Community Shop and Café, Devon – Having successfully set up a community shop and post office in their village hall when their local shop closed and become a private house, villagers at Exbourne with Jacobstowe set up an Industrial and Provident Society to fund a new-build shop.

Of the £296 000 they need for the project, around £60 000 will be provided by local people buying shares and making donations. The remainder is coming from a wide range of statutory bodies, local and national grant makers.

Although only 20% of the funding is locally raised, it clearly demonstrates local support and commitment. This shows other funders that the project is likely to succeed and makes it easier for them to support the venture.

In summary

- 🐣 You need long term capital finance to get set up and ready to go.
- 🐣 Working capital can often be funded via a bank overdraft.
- 🐣 Social entrepreneurs can often apply for grants to help them get started;
- 🐣 You can apply for grants as a social entrepreneur.
- 🐣 Grants can come from all kinds of sources.
- 🐣 Use the CAMPARI test to check you've covered everything when seeking bank loans.
- 🐣 Community ownership of shops and pubs means they become more sustainable financially, keeping those communities alive;

Find out more

Social Enterprise London – free downloads	sel.org.uk/publications
Fundraising tips – Directory of Social Change	dsc.org.uk
Grants for individuals – Unlimited	unltd.org
Community Development Finance Association	cdfa.org.uk
Rural community shops – Plunkett Foundation	plunkett.co.uk

Part Four
How to Grow

10

Selling and the Social Enterprise

'Do you want to spend the rest of your life selling sugared water or do you want a chance to change the world?'

Steve Jobs when persuading John Sculley of PepsiCo to join Apple as CEO

How to open doors

If there is one skill you need to succeed in any kind of enterprise, it is the ability to sell. If you can sell, everything else becomes possible. If you cannot, then however good you are at what you do, your success will depend on others finding and supporting you.

As a social entrepreneur, you have a great advantage over many of the employed sales people you encounter in your everyday life. That is the huge passion you feel for what it is you are doing and the difference it is making. It is far harder to get excited about selling sofas, fridges or life insurance!

It is also fair to say that many people have hang ups about selling. They see it as some kind of dark art, used to persuade perfectly sensible people to do things that on reflection they'd rather not. Indeed you may have experienced for yourself the desperate and often embarrassing attempts of the door to door home improvements salesman, trying to persuade you to buy his nice double glazed units. Selling within the context of a social enterprise is nothing like that at all.

What are you selling?

As a social entrepreneur you are probably selling lots of different things to very different groups of people. In fact true sustainability is often only achieved when you can successfully identify all of your different potential customer groups and sell to them effectively.

First though, you need to consider how to sell. In the next chapter you will see that not all customers are obvious as such. Some may even be people you think you are helping out, when actually you are providing them with something they would pay for, if asked in the right way. It's a lot about mindset and being aware of the benefits you can provide and their value in real terms.

Opening doors

So, not all of your potential customers will see themselves as such. They are busy managing their own affairs and need you to gently introduce them to the benefits you can bring. All people prioritise their time and often you have to introduce the idea that doing business with you is a good idea. How do you do this? Here is a process you can follow that will help you gain people's attention.

Essentially, the sales process can be simply summarised by the mnemonic AIDA:

→ **Awareness** – getting noticed by your prospective customer.
→ **Interest** – helping them see that there is an opportunity.
→ **Desire** – making it appealing to do business with you.
→ **Action** – closing the deal or at least committing them to some follow up.

Marketing, which is covered in Chapter 14, is the process by which larger organisations raise awareness and generate enquiries. If you have a large organisation, you will need to spend money on marketing. However, if you are starting something small, you will be marketing mostly by word of mouth.

So here are seven steps that will open doors for you:

1. **Decide** what it is you are selling and who has the greatest potential.
2. **Find** the people your research suggests will be most interested.
3. **Extract** from that list the five with whom you can claim any connection.
4. **Identify** something you have in common with each of them.
5. **Write** a letter or email to summarise why meeting you is in their interests.
6. **Phone** to follow up and suggest a meeting.
7. **Agree** something with them, either a date or a time to call again.

As well as the process, you also need the right attitude. People naturally assume that when they are approached with any offer, the value to the seller is going to be greater than the value to the buyer. Imagine a 'Big Issue' seller with one copy of the magazine left.

He wants to sell it so he can go and do something else after a morning of rebuffs and rejections on the street. But the buyer of that final copy needs to feel that the combination of a good read and helping someone in need is greater. In fact done properly, the last copy is easier to sell because there is a scarcity of copies.

So when you are opening dialogue with your potential customers, you must:

→ focus on what's important to them, not you about the proposed transaction;
→ talk about their needs not your own;
→ avoid seeking sympathy – instead describe benefits.

What works

People like to talk about themselves, make it easy for them by being a good listener. Tell them enough about your proposition and then let them tell you why it might be useful to them to do business with you.

How to say it like it is – features and benefits

Having looked at how to open doors, it's now time to think a little deeper about what it is you are selling. People do not buy anything for what it is, but for what it does. In other words, everything you buy is purchased because of what you think it will do for you. For example, you choose your:

→ clothes more for your taste in fashion than the need to keep warm;
→ career more for job satisfaction than earning potential;
→ life partner because you love them, not for their genetic make-up.

These are obvious when you think about it, but put yourself in the shoes of the person selling each to you:

→ The assistant in the fashion store tells you how good you'll look, rather than giving you the thermal performance of each garment.
→ Telling you how much money you'll earn alone won't persuade you to change employers.
→ A dating agency will focus on common interests and tastes, rather than complementing your genetic make up to create the best possible babies.

In each case, you buy because of the benefits to you (looking good, being happy at work and being in love) not because of the features.

When you are selling the idea of supporting your social enterprise, or even just taking part in a campaign, you need to focus on the benefits not the features.

Using features and benefits

Clearly different people will perceive different benefits to be most important. That's why it's vital to engage people in a focused conversation to find out what they are likely to value most.

Imagine you are promoting Fit Club CIC, the example used in Chapter 7, an imaginary organisation that provides personal training to older people. There are two key benefits for the client. First it increases life expectancy and secondly it improves life quality because you remain active for longer. However, your clients might view this differently.

For example, if you did not ask what they considered most important, you might find yourself promoting longevity to someone recently bereaved. They might be keen to get fitter so they can get out and about, but be disinterested in living longer as they are still grieving for their lost partner.

Equally, someone who has never been motivated by exercise and watches TV all day might take up your service because they want to live longer. You can see that it is really important to ask the right questions to find out what people really want to achieve. You simply cannot assume that others share the same outlook on life as you.

Why street fundraising is such hard work

When someone shakes a collecting tin under your nose, or even approaches you with clipboard and pen, you are more likely to say no than yes. If you do say yes, you'll only put small change in the tin and likely as not, stop the direct debit set up by the 'chugger' you met on the High Street.

Street fundraising is only done because:

→ there is a constant flow of people to approach;
→ the cost of standing in the street is very low (especially if you use volunteers);
→ every now and then someone comes along with a real interest in the cause and gives generously.

Many people find the process intrusive, annoying and some only give because you have embarrassed them. They are given little opportunity to see the benefit to them in supporting the cause. All they can see is what's in it for the cause.

Compare this with 'big gift' fundraising, where potential donors are:

→ carefully researched and selected for some link or connection with your cause;
→ sensitively approached, often through someone you have found who has agreed to make an introduction;
→ nurtured and encouraged to find out more at a pace they find comfortable;
→ flattered into feeling wanted and helped to see a range of opportunities;
→ taken on 'seeing is believing' visits to get close to the need;
→ introduced to existing donors.

In short, the big gift fundraiser builds a relationship and comes to understand the donor's needs. They talk benefits not features and that's why they achieve much more than street collectors.

What works

In today's world, you achieve more by shaking hands than you ever can by shaking tins.

Buying motives

So, to look at why this is – and it applies to almost any decision we make – we need to consider buying motives. These are quite simply the reasons we buy and inevitably the decision will be based on one or more of the following:

→ **Security** – is it safe and going to be there when I need it next?
→ **Performance** – will it do well, better for me than the alternatives?
→ **Appearance** – does it look good and moreover, will it make me look good?
→ **Convenience** – is the process going to be easy or are there lots of hurdles?
→ **Economy** – does it represent good value for money?
→ **Durability** – how long will it last and when will it go out of fashion?

If you think in terms of buying motives when structuring your sales proposition, you'll find that you automatically think in terms of benefits not features. Use the mnemonic SPACED to help you.

Imagine, for example, that you are negotiating a contract to take green waste from your local council for a composting project. The decision to agree to let you have the material, (perhaps even to pay you what disposal currently costs) might look like this:

- ➞ **Security** – 'I can see how the trainees are supervised so there is no risk of accidents on our site.'
- ➞ **Performance** – 'It's going to be a lot easier than sending it to landfill.'
- ➞ **Appearance** – 'it will make a great press story about how we're supporting social enterprise.'
- ➞ **Convenience** – 'I just ring and they say they'll collect within 48 hrs.'
- ➞ **Economy** – 'it will actually cost us less.'
- ➞ **Durability** – 'they've been around for a year and seem to know what they're doing.'

No single one of these thoughts passing through the mind of the Council Officer making the decision is in itself sufficient to prompt a change of behaviour. Add them together and there is a compelling argument for change. That's how buying decisions are made.

What works

Help people to see how dealing with you will satisfy several different buying motives. The stronger the motive to buy, the better the deal you'll be able to strike.

How to get commitment

Most people find it difficult to ask for commitment for or to put it crudely, close the sale. When you are in business to make a difference, having to be persuasive, pushy even, just doesn't come naturally. This feels even worse if your career to date has been in a non-commercial environment. You are a social entrepreneur because you want to help people, not make them feel uncomfortable.

But in reality it is human nature to prevaricate, to delay and to defer decisions. What you have to do is to make it as easy as possible for people to make the decision you'd like them to make.

Clearly much of the skill of closing sales is in the way you quantify the various benefits. The more the value to the other person exceeds the cost, then the easier it is to say yes. But for now, let's focus on technique. How do you persuade someone to say yes, when although they are clearly interested, commitment just doesn't seem to be forthcoming?

It's all about technique and the good news is, that handled correctly, people do not feel pressured or annoyed. Instead they feel reassured that you have helped them to make the decision. It is also not about pressuring people, although you do have to gently put them on the spot.

 What works

Never ask anyone to make a decision that in their situation you would not make yourself. If it appears to be wrong for them, say so and move on.

Here are some ways to help people make the commitment you're asking of them.

Ask them

You'd be surprised how many people working in sales are reluctant to ask for the business. It's because they fear rejection and believe that prompting a 'no' means they've lost the deal. In fact the opposite is true. Only when people say no, and you ask them why, do you hear what concerns remain. Once you know what the barriers are, you can work out how to overcome them.

The other, far simpler reason for asking for the sale is that even the most enthusiastic buyer is unlikely to stop you in full flow and say; 'yes, OK let's do it.' Instead they will let you ramble on, becoming increasingly frustrated and rapidly losing interest.

➡ Do ask the direct question.
➡ Do not take no as no; instead ask why and deal with the objection.

Create urgency

Your timescale might be different to your customer's. The art is to help them see that by doing it now, they will benefit more than if they delay. In fact creating urgency means that if they delay too long, they might miss the opportunity.

Urgency can be created because:

➡ you have only capacity for one more client;

➡ your project is seasonal and to delay a month means waiting a year;

➡ only one person can be the first sponsor;

➡ prices are rising but you have one left in stock at the old price.

There is almost always some urgency, even if only that once committed, your customer will not have the budget to invest in anything else.

➡ Do try to build urgency into your offer.

➡ Do not fib though; if there is no urgency, try another tack.

Try before you buy

Imagine you are running an animal rescue centre. You want to find homes for a litter of kittens. Offer to take the kitten back if the couple pondering will change their mind. It means they take it home with them today. Once there they'll fall for its cuteness and appeal and never think of changing their mind (naturally you've already checked their suitability before making the offer).

The same 'try before you buy' approach can be used in many situations. Rather than trying to sell the full programme, you simply market an opportunity to try. Because the customer can see that they can say no later without losing face, they are more likely to say yes now.

➡ Do structure your service so people can try it out at low risk/cost first.

➡ Do not simply offer a 'money back guarantee' that commits you too much!

Offer alternatives

The classic way to get commitment is to offer an alternative. The professional salesperson will make that choice between something specific and something more general. For example, would you like a green one or another colour?

That's because if they want green they'll choose it. But if they wanted red and you offered yellow, they'd say no to both. It'd actually quite difficult to say 'no I don't want one at all'. Easier to say, 'I'm more interested in another colour.' Then you can ask them which colour and they feel obliged to choose one, or raise a specific objection you can deal with.

➡ Do always offer alternatives.
➡ Don't keep doing it until you narrow down their choice. That's irritating!

Put yourself in their shoes

The reality is that the proposition you are discussing will form a relatively small part of the life and work of the person you're selling to. Not only must you keep things in proportion, but you must also try to see things from their perspective.

If you can't quite see things as they do, ask them to help you by explaining what else is going on with them and where your offer fits. By questioning the perception they describe, you can bring them closer to the commitment you're seeking.

➡ Do make the effort to see things from the other person's perspective.

➡ Do not tell anyone they're wrong, when actually you just see things differently.

What works

If you run out of things to say, ask a question. Their answer will probably help you get the interview back on track.

Selling pitfalls and how to avoid them

To conclude this chapter on selling, here are a few common mistakes and how to avoid them. You've worked hard to take on board the points made so far, so here's an opportunity to take a lighter hearted look at selling.

Don't be too cheap

If you don't have a good grasp of your enterprise's costs, you can easily get talked into selling too cheap; promising the impossible and because you enjoy the popularity, agreeing seems to buy you, saying yes to anything.

TIP: Know how far you can go before you start and say no if pushed too far. Often people 'try it on' and once you've said no as if you mean it, will relent and agree something you can actually achieve.

Don't criticise

If you tell someone that what they're currently doing is silly, you are really telling them that they're silly. It can be really tempting to point out the failings of what's being done right now because to you, the difference is obvious and the opportunity huge.

TIP: Always ask your prospect to explain the pros and cons of what they currently do. Dig around a little and let them pick up on the shortcomings. Properly prompted, people usually spot the opportunity. Help them find it for themselves.

Don't over-promise

It is all too easy to agree to crazy deadlines and impossible outputs, especially if you are bidding for a public sector contract. These often start with the results of a survey, plus a consultant's recommendation as to what is needed. There is no guarantee that anyone believes the task is achievable. Don't promise what you can't deliver.

TIP: If you're confronted by an invitation to tender for something you don't think is possible, suggest something different. You know you can't deliver what is asked for, so have nothing to lose by suggesting what you can do and feel deep down is going to be better.

In summary, selling is all about helping people see opportunities and agree to explore them together. It's about shared commitment and shared success. Selling should not be adversarial; selling should actually be fun!

In summary

- Selling is easier for social entrepreneurs because they passionately believe in what they are doing.
- Before you start selling, you need to identify every one of your potential customer groups.
- People need to become aware, then interested in what you have to offer.
- Closing the deal is not about being pushy, more a case of making it easy to say yes.
- People buy what things do, not what they are.
- The bigger the deal the more focused your selling needs to be.
- Use the mnemonic SPACED to remember the six buying motives.
- We all make mistakes when selling. Learn from your mistakes.

Find out more

Social Enterprise London   sel.org.uk/publications

11

The Customer Conundrum

'Touch your customers and you're half way there.'
Estee Lauder

The difference between customers and clients

People running social enterprises, charities and public sector organisations often confuse the words customer and client. You might say the words are interchangeable and at times they are, but if you're going to be commercially successful, you need to clearly differentiate between the two.

If you check a dictionary, you'll find that:

→ customers are people who buy goods or services;
→ clients are people receiving the benefits of a product or service.

You may find it simplifies things to get into the habit of calling:

→ clients the people you have set your enterprise up to help and,
→ customers the people who pay you money.

This will help you differentiate between service delivery and income generation.

Just suppose you make play equipment, swings, slides and roundabouts. The public park needs new equipment and the Council look around for suppliers. Because the council are making the purchase, they are the customer. But as the officers and members of the Council are unlikely to play on the swings and slide themselves, they are not the beneficiaries. Your clients then are the local kids who will use the park.

If you've set up a social enterprise, your clients might well form your 'community of interest'. They're the people you care about and want to support. They're the people in whom you invest a significant proportion of your profits. Close to them might be some of your customers. The boundary between the two groups can get blurred; indeed it can move.

For example, let's suppose you run a counselling and psychotherapy service. You're set up as a social enterprise and invest your profits in funding your staff to work with people unable to afford the fees. It could be that they are workless and that the NHS funded therapy services are inadequate. Your enterprise funds itself by providing the same services to people able to pay their way. For every three paying customers, you can afford to support one non-paying client.

It's all straightforward until one of your paying customers loses their job and cannot afford to continue. At the same time, one of your non-paying clients wins £5000 at bingo. Their roles could now reverse.

In this situation, the only difference between your clients and customers is their ability to pay. This contrasts markedly with the playground example, in which client and customer are clearly different. So:

- some clients will pay and so can also be considered customers;
- some clients will never pay, but are funded by others who are customers.

 What works

Always clearly differentiate between your customers and your clients. Your customers are important because they make your organisation sustainable. Your clients, on the other hand, are the people you really set out to help.

Reality is often less straightforward

If only life was as simple as in the two examples above. In reality things are usually far more complicated, which is why it's important to make clear distinctions between the two groups. Few counselling and therapy services exist on income from paying customers alone.

Most, if they're going to be effective in combating social problems, will also be funded by local government, grant making trusts and perhaps even the health service. These subsidies are important in that they enable an organisation to deliver the services it wants to deliver, to those it wants to help, from the outset.

The danger is that you remain reliant on subsidy and fail to strive for self sufficiency. That's not surprising when you need to deliver perhaps 200 paid for counselling sessions to earn £10000 and a single grant maker might give you that for making one simple funding application. However, no business should become over-reliant on one customer; things can quickly become sticky when you lose them.

Here's a more complicated, perhaps realistic scenario to illustrate the complexity of some organisations customer/client mix. Assume you're running a timber recycling enterprise. You work from a large rented unit, collect waste timber from building sites, shop fitters and the like. You provide employment for people recovering from long term mental illness, some of whom make garden furniture from the timber you collect. Others chop and bundle the waste timber into firewood, after first picking out the re-useable wood for sale on to hobbyists.

Your clients are your service users. They are referred to you by a number of health and social services agencies who give you some core funding to run your organisation.

You also have a larger number of customers, or potential customers, than you might first realise. For example:

- **Builders** have to pay for rubbish to be taken off site. They'll pay you to take it away instead because it's being re-used and creating opportunities for disadvantaged people.
- **Employment organisations** will pay you for the training and experience you provide.
- **Garden centres** will stock the furniture you make because there's a good story attached that will encourage people to buy it.
- **Hobby woodworkers** will buy timber you have salvaged because it costs less than new and enables them to use recycled materials.
- **Householders** will buy firewood from you because it is convenient and environmentally friendly.
- **Local businesses** might provide you with tools and even volunteer staff, as part of their 'corporate social responsibility' activity.
- **Your landlord** might also be a customer, because allowing you to occupy otherwise empty premises (perhaps scheduled for redevelopment) means the landlord saves the business rates otherwise payable on empty premises.

Furthermore, it's quite easy to work out the starting point for your negotiations with each of these groups:

- Look at what waste companies charge for skips and see what builders might be paying to have taken away the timber you have been removing for free.
- Look on public tender websites to see what employment organisations receive for the work experience placements you can provide.

➥ Garden centres, like most retailers, will calculate their selling price by doubling the buying price and adding VAT.

➥ Your local DIY store will sell timber. How much cheaper do you need to be to compete?

➥ Householders buy firewood from filling stations and garden centres. Pitch your price a little lower.

➥ Teambuilding training is expensive to buy. Volunteering for you might save that expense. Don't be afraid to do the sums.

What works

You can start to negotiate only when you have a good idea what the alternatives cost your customers.

Catch 22 is a social enterprise that publishes a youth magazine in London. It is also a communications agency, providing design and copywriting services. The work is carried out by creative young people who are supported by bursaries to train and gain experience with the organisation.

The organisation has two groups of clients. Those who it helps get their careers off the ground and readers of the magazine. Both are often from disadvantaged backgrounds that tend to exclude them from opportunity.

Customers include sponsors such as 'The Economist' and 'BBC Magazines', who fund bursaries and advertisers in the magazine.

Who pays and who says – striking a balance

So you are beginning to form an idea that the things you've perhaps done for free actually have a value. Perhaps you can't realistically go to people you already deal with and start asking them to pay. But you can agree with them what it would cost if they did pay. This will make sure they value what you do more highly. It also helps them to see that whilst they don't pay, future customers will.

You can quite comfortably have two identical customers, one who you've had a while who doesn't pay and one who has been recently recruited who does. Moreover both would understand this if they knew and arguably, there's no harm in telling them. In fact it's usually better to tell people things they might consider controversial if they hear it from a third party.

Being a vector

Vector is not a commonly used word, but it does accurately define the relationship many social enterprises have with their customers and clients. A vector is something that conveys or carries something from one place to another. But it is much more than, say a parcel delivery service. Vectors carry things to places they could not get to on their own. For example, bees are vectors in the way they carry pollen from plant to plant. The flower is colourful to attract the bee, for without the bee pollination would not happen.

It's the same with fruit. The only way fruit trees can colonise a wider area is by wrapping their seeds in tasty fruits that get eaten and then dropped some way away in a convenient mound of manure.

Many social enterprises act as very successful vectors. They have unique access to disadvantaged communities and groups and can use that to 'carry in' messages, initiatives and activities on behalf of others who alone, would not have the credibility or wherewithal to make an impact.

The Respect Group is a social enterprise that works with both young people and ex-offenders. One of its projects involves taking ex-offenders into schools to explain to youngsters the realities of life with a criminal record.

The message that crime doesn't pay would not be taken seriously if delivered in school by teachers, police officers or the local Council. Instead, The Respect Group acts as a vector, funded to deliver the message on behalf of a number of statutory agencies.

The funders know the cost to society of keeping someone in prison and of the almost inevitable period of worklessness that follows their release. The Respect Group know that they can reduce the risk of future offending very effectively. They are paid to convey the message.

Using ex-offenders to help them has had an added benefit in that it helped build the confidence and self-esteem of one of the organisation's core client groups.

Seeing your organisation as a vector can help you identify new potential customers. Clearly your vision and values will dictate who you might allow to access your client group. They have to be providing or promising something you feel will improve the lot of your clients.

Client power

As you seek to strengthen your relationship with existing customers, as well perhaps as identify and recruit new ones, your client group has a vital role to play.

The more accurately you can determine the level of interest and the likely impact, then the better positioned you are to negotiate a deal with your customers. If you've tendered to deliver community projects in the past, you'll know that funders often have a very good idea of what they need to see happen. Most recognised social or environmental needs have been quantified.

For example, if you're setting up a community transport enterprise, the financial cost of the rural isolation you're setting out to overcome will have been calculated by a number of agencies. More doctor home visits, more people supported by benefits because they cannot travel to get work, all might be attributable to a lack of suitable public transport.

You can argue for some of the funding your project will save, to help set up and run the operation. This will be all the more powerful and effective if you have surveyed the communities your transport scheme will serve and have actual examples of people who will clearly benefit from the service.

Good ways to involve your client group in putting together your commercial argument include:

➡ survey forms that collate actual hard evidence of need and the impact of the investment you're seeking;
➡ video clips of potential beneficiaries explaining what the project will mean to them;
➡ beneficiary focus groups attended by potential funders/ sponsors who hear for themselves what can be achieved;
➡ local service provider endorsements detailing the likely financial savings.

What works

The more you can illustrate the difference you plan to make with real people's stories and commitment, the easier it will be to win financial support.

Selling both the tangible and intangible

Typically, a social enterprise will be selling both tangible and intangible benefits. Tangible benefits are things you can easily measure and intangible things you might find quite hard to measure, but which have a value all the same. For example:

Tangible products/services might include:

→ food and drink in a community café;
→ a trainee coming off benefits to take on a part time job;
→ the running costs of a public building that passes into community ownership.

Because these can be easily measured, it's relatively easy to justify the price should you need to. A community organisation taking over a building say, might agree a reducing grant from the building's former council owner over the first three years to contribute to the running costs. Because the council would be paying all the costs if they had retained the building, negotiating transitional support should be relatively straightforward – in concept at least.

Intangible products/services might include:

→ a reduction in youth offending;
→ an increase in life expectancy;
→ fewer single parent families.

In each of these scenarios, you cannot prove that:

→ the youngsters you worked with would have otherwise committed crimes;
→ the people whose fitness you improve would not have lived until 90 anyway;

➡ the users of your relationship counselling service would not have become reconciled without your intervention.

But equally, others cannot prove that you are not bringing these benefits. When selling intangibles, it is even more important than ever to encourage your customer to do the sums for themselves. That way, they will appear more credible than if you do the calculations and encourage others to believe them.

If selling intangibles sounds a little dubious to you, reflect for a moment on the insurance industry. People buy insurance to protect them financially from risk. If you buy life insurance and stay alive, or skiing insurance and do not need to be repatriated on a stretcher, you do not complain about the cost of the policy.

Techniques used to sell insurance that may with a little adaptation work for you include encouraging your prospective customer to:

➡ imagine the worst possible happening without the insurance;
➡ recognise their duty to protect those weaker than themselves;
➡ appreciate how others benefit from the peace of mind the insurance buys.

 What works

The harder a benefit is to see in real terms, the more you have to encourage others to bring the possibility to life in their imagination.

Social return on investment – opportunity or threat?

The concept of social return on investment (SROI) has already been covered, but it needs to be visited again here. That's because some of your most lucrative customers will be those buying in to the social return they can reap by investing in what you do.

SROI is an intangible product. You cannot guarantee that your clients would have behaved differently had you not worked with them. Instead you have to build your argument to say that with as little doubt as possible, you are saving others having to spend, by doing what you do.

People in the public sector are increasingly using SROI to support their own budget bids. For example, a police force might quote published research that calculates the cost of a life of crime to seek a tiny proportion of that sum to work with youngsters at risk of offending and reduce that risk.

Diehard private sector folk might see SROI as being soft and fluffy. Politicians might argue the same, if casting doubt will help them reduce expenditure now. The fact is though, that using SROI to support and justify claims for funding is going to become increasingly important. Few true social enterprises can survive on income from commercial activity alone. Most need a share of the money their work is saving others. Indeed, looked at logically, why shouldn't they have a share of what they can save? It can represent excellent value for money.

The biggest challenge with SROI is that you are asking people to pay you now, a proportion of the money you're going to save them needing to spend much later. We live in a world where too many people focus on reducing spend today, because funding tomorrow will be someone else's problem!

In summary

◉ Customers buy things and clients benefit from them. Some clients are also customers, but not all customers are clients. Understand the difference in your enterprise.

◉ If you look closely, you might have more different customer groups than you first thought.

◉ Know what things cost and negotiate with a mindset that says you're doing business, not asking for favours.

◉ If you can act as a vector, delivering change more effectively than the sponsor could themselves, they can become your customers and pay for the value you deliver.

◉ Involve your client group in illustrating the importance and value of what you do.

◉ Intangibles need selling differently to tangibles – with more finesse.

◉ SROI is an intangible and should be sold as such.

Find out more

Catch 22   catch22mag.com
The Respect Group   therespectgroup.org

12

Managing Money

'Money is like sixth sense without which you cannot make a complete use of the other five.'

W Somerset Maugham, *Of Human Bondage*, 1915

Keeping your finger on the pulse – good cash flow

O ur relationship with money is deep and complex. If you are a person who cares deeply about people, environment and equality, then managing money may not be top of your list of priorities. But like it or not, money is vital to the sustainability of any organisation. Wages and bills have to be paid and without a healthy cash flow, you jeopardise the work you set out to do and the very difference you hope to make.

The importance of cash flow was introduced in Chapter 9. It is commonly described as the lifeblood of your organisation. But how can you measure it and more importantly, keep it healthy without compromising the ideals that led you to this point?

Big businesses often manage their cash flow in a harsh and at times brutal way. They make demands on their suppliers such as:

→ just in time delivery – so they only need to buy what they need, when they need it;
→ rigorous quality standards that mean only the very best is accepted and the rest rejected;
→ substantial discounting in return for volume commitment;
→ sale or return – so if it's not used it can be sent back and a refund obtained;
→ extended credit – so that goods are only paid for long after they have been used and the income from that use banked.

So if, for example, you are producing and packing salads for a supermarket chain, you can find yourself very much at the beck and call of your customer. If the weather turns cold, orders might be cancelled. If your quality slips, consignments are rejected and once your produce is in the supermarket, it will have been purchased and paid for by shoppers perhaps three months before you get paid.

Managing money flowing in

You may not have the clout or desire to be as tough on your customers as some major corporations are on theirs. But you do need to be realistic and businesslike. The first thing to do is work out how long on average people keep you waiting for money. It's called 'debtor days' and for many comes as a nasty surprise when they realise how long people are taking to pay.

This is how you work it out:

$$\frac{\text{sum outstanding}}{\text{Annual turnover}} \times 365 = \text{Debtor days}$$

So if your income is £600 000pa and at the moment you are waiting for payment of invoices totalling £100 000, you can work out that on average people are taking 60 days to pay you.

$$\frac{£100\,000}{£600\,000} \times 365 = 60$$

You can see at a glance that if people paid you twice as fast, ie within the month, you would have on average £50 000 more in your bank account. If your organisation runs on an overdraft, that money is costing you money to borrow.

What happens

If people are slow to chase the payments due to them they can find themselves with insufficient money in the bank to pay staff and suppliers.

You can manage the money coming into your organisation effectively and gently, without compromising your caring values. Here are some tips to help you:

→ Print 'payment within 14 days please' on your invoices rather than 28.

→ Phone to check that the invoice is in the payment run when it falls due (large organisations genuinely do lose invoices in the system!).

→ Negotiate staged payments for large projects and from statutory funders.

→ Be thorough when making grant claims and include all the evidence needed.

Keeping on top of your money flow in sounds easy, but in reality, when you might be spending a lot of time dealing with day to day challenges, it's all too easy to let things slip.

What works

Set aside a fixed time each week to review your finances, raise invoices and chase payments.

Managing the money flowing out

Spending money is easy; good fun even. Spending money at work never feels quite the same as spending it at home. For one thing your enterprise probably has a bigger budget to play with and for another, it's somehow less personal. It goes without saying though, that there are only two ways to increase profits in any organisation:

→ sell more;
→ spend less.

If as a social entrepreneur your profit is to be invested in making a difference, then you have added incentive to be sensible with your money.

Just as being paid late harms your cash flow, so too can paying bills too early. Worse though is to overspend then delay paying the bills until the last possible moment. You can kid yourself by delaying payment that you're making money when actually you are not.

Imagine that your monthly outgoings to suppliers total £10 000 and you now need to pay last month's invoices. Your overdraft limit is £10 000 and you started this month with a credit balance at the bank of £5000. You can see that you could pay all of your bills and end up using half of the overdraft.

But just suppose you decide you need to buy a van, pay £8000 cash for it and simply put off paying your bills for an additional month. You still stay within your overdraft limit, but now you have slipped a month with suppliers who you could not pay if they demanded the money they are owed.

Had you decided instead to finance the van over perhaps a year (something the dealer could probably have easily arranged) you would have been able to pay your bills and have the van. By stretching your supplier payments you may jeopardise your trading relationship with them. More critically, you have dramatically reduced your ability to cope should your cash flow take an unforeseen knock in the months ahead.

You can calculate how long on average it takes you to pay your bills as follows:

$$\frac{\text{bills outstanding}}{\text{Annual spend}} \times 365 = \text{Creditor days}$$

The calculation is not quite as straightforward as that for debtor days. This is because you have to exclude things like your payroll. However, if you are a trading organisation, or have a trading arm, you can apply the calculation to just that part of the organisation.

You need to manage the money flowing out of your organisation with the same care you manage the money flowing in. Here are some tips to help you:

→ Agree at time of purchase when you will make payment:
  • you can negotiate discounts if able to pay quickly;
  • if you need extended credit discuss this up front.
→ Consider your cash flow forecast and time purchases for when you know you'll have the cash to pay for them.
→ Don't be afraid to pay small suppliers quickly and make the bigger ones wait a little longer. Like you, smaller suppliers usually have a tighter cash flow.

 What works

Make payments out in batches rather than as and when the bills come in. Time this to coincide with reviewing the money others owe to you. Link them in your life, as well as in your cash flow.

Monitoring cash flow

Few organisations have an even cash flow. Most encounter peaks and troughs of both expenditure and income. A good way to monitor cash flow is to create a cash flow spreadsheet (see example in Chapter 9) and expand it to cover your whole enterprise.

To avoid making it too complicated, just list major items or group categories of spending or income together. Project the calculation forward so you can see the impact on the fluctuations on your bank balance.

As well as regularly updating the figures, replacing estimates with actuals, you can look ahead and see how you can influence cash flow. You might:

→ delay making purchases at a time of year when income is low;
→ look for additional income opportunities during months when you predict low demand for services;
→ negotiate with customers and suppliers payment profiles that even out peaks and troughs and make cash flow easier to manage.

Budgets

When you prepare a business plan you create an annual budget that details where the money will come from and where it will go. Often, these are guesstimates, put together to reassure yourself and others that the plan is going to work.

When you get started, it pays to look again at your annual budget and actually create a monthly expenditure budget for the major areas of activity. These could include:

➞ temporary staff;
➞ materials you need to do your work;
➞ IT;
➞ marketing.

The key is to create and manage budgets for the things that can and may change. Salaries and rent are pretty much pre-defined so providing they are counted in your cash flow, you don't need to budget for them separately. But marketing and IT are areas where it does pay to have a budget and record your spend against it. This is because without a defined budget:

➞ you are more likely to spend more on an ad-hoc basis;
➞ your spend may be made at the best time of year;
➞ unplanned expenditure usually delivers less value than planned spend.

Traditionally in the public sector, budgets set but not spent by the end of the financial year were returned to the Treasury. This meant that people would sometimes go on a spending spree at the end of the year to avoid having their unspent budget taken back.

As a social entrepreneur you probably do not live with this same constraint.

What works

Setting budgets for the different parts of your enterprise helps you spend wisely. And remember you don't HAVE to spend it all!

Costing, pricing and why full cost recovery is vital

Whilst a social enterprise might form a trading division or subsidiary of a charity, it is not a charity nor should it behave like one. That's not to say it should not have a strong social purpose because of course it should. It's more that a social enterprise should meet its social purpose in a sustainable, businesslike way.

As a social entrepreneur you will want to deliver lasting change. Too often charities simply see the need, fundraise to meet the need, and then they simply repeat the cycle. You, on the other hand, want to meet the need in a way that is economically viable and may well involve your beneficiaries in carrying out that economic activity.

Costing

Knowing what things really cost you is vitally important. It's not good practice to simply throw all your costs into the same pot. Equally, if your organisation is very small, it would be wrong to become obsessed with cost centres for each and every aspect of what you do.

The pragmatic middle ground is where you need to be, with your most significant activities fully costed and closely monitored, but with stuff on the fringe grouped together. For example, if you managed a community shop, you'd want to know:

→ What it costs you a month before you open the door. Rent, finance costs, insurance and employed staff. These are your fixed costs.

➡ Which sections of the shop delivered the greatest margin and the least waste.

➡ If part of the business had specific costs attached to it, for example home delivery or a café, you'd need to work out how many vegetable boxes or cups or afternoon teas you need to provide to cover the additional cost.

Monitoring the performance of your enterprise week by week or month by month means you can quickly see what's working and what's not. You can then act if things are not performing. It's also far easier to measure the impact of any marketing you do, because you can see how sales and profits rise or fall.

What works

If part of your business is a separate cost centre, share the targets and even a percentage of the profit with the staff running it. They probably have the biggest opportunity to make it succeed as well as the most to lose if it fails.

Lastly, what about the cause you set out to support? How should you cost that activity? In fact you should cost this as carefully as your more enterprising activities. That's because:

➡ If you know what it costs you know how much of it you can do.

➡ If it's costed, sponsors, supporters and others can know exactly what their money can buy.

➡ If you cost something, you can quantify it in your business plan.

Pricing

There are essentially two ways to determine your selling price for anything. The first is to calculate the cost and add a margin. The second is to start with the market price and set your own price depending on your market position. The one thing both methods should have in common is that with the exception of 'loss leaders' (products sold at less than cost price to entice new customers in) you should not sell anything at less than cost price. Nor should you cap the price if circumstances place you in a particularly strong market position.

Think about ice cream. A trade carton of choc-ices from the wholesaler has a standard price. This will give both the manufacturer and wholesaler a profit. Two retailers buy a box each.

One runs a convenience store and the other runs an ice cream van. The storekeeper sells ice creams alongside newspapers, sweets and cigarettes. She sells her choc ices at a higher price than say a supermarket for two reasons. This is because her customers are willing to pay a small premium for the convenience of shopping locally.

The second pays the same price, but sells at a far higher price. His price to the customer is 30% higher than even the convenience store, yet he has a queue waiting to buy for much of the day. This is because he has an ice cream van parked between the car park and beach. Again, nobody complains because to walk any further from the beach means getting dressed and losing their spot on the beach.

Now not all social enterprises sell ice cream but all have the opportunity to pitch their price at or near the market level, rather than simply add a margin to their costs. Even if you are selling 'social outcomes' to a public sector funder, you can at least look for ways to increase the price above the lowest possible commodity price for the service you deliver.

Most publicly funded programmes have target success rates. If you can exceed these, or add value in some other way, you have the opportunity to differentiate yourself against alternative providers and command a premium.

When pricing your products or services as a social enterprise, remember the six reasons people buy. (The mnemonic SPACED is explained in Chapter 10). As a social enterprise, you have a number of advantages. These include:

→ People like to buy from socially responsible organizations.
→ You invest profits in doing good, not getting rich.
→ Buying from you may help less advantaged people to get on in life.
→ You might offer something your competitors cannot.

Wayland Radio is a community radio station in Norfolk. It is also a social enterprise, needing to generate a significant proportion of its running costs to stay on air.

Station manager Dave Hatherly sells advertising to local businesses, which he makes as easy as possible by providing a variety of affordable packages, while working with local

traders to write and produce the ads as well. He uses professional voice artists to give a professional sound.

Ads are competitively priced, but cost more per thousand
listeners than larger commercial stations. However, for most,
advertising with the bigger stations means reaching people
outside their trading area. Advertising with Wayland Radio
provides better value, targets a hard to reach rural community
and supports a unique and valuable service.

Full cost recovery

If you work with people in the charity sector, you'll be familiar
with the phrase 'full cost recovery'. It's as much a philosophy
as a methodology, prompted by the fact that it is traditionally
quite difficult for service delivery charities to persuade the
commissioners of services to contribute to their overhead
costs.

Most contracts will embrace the direct costs associated with
service delivery, but that can leave a gap in the organisation's
finances. Of course general fundraising can cover overhead
costs, but the principle is that then the commissioner is getting
more than they are willing to pay for.

Representatives from the charity sector and Government nego-
tiated a common methodology that charities could use to
attribute core costs to service delivery costs.

The principle holds true for every organisation, including
yours. Overhead costs need to taken into account when costing
and pricing the products and services you deliver.

Getting paid – how to ask and when to chase

Nobody likes asking for money. Even the most hardened business person can find chasing an overdue payment daunting. It is one of the few situations in commerce where people are not always totally truthful with each other. There are a host of stock answers that people give to avoid telling you the truth; that right now, they haven't got the money to pay you.

What works

If your cash flow means you can't pay a bill when it's due, the best strategy is always to be proactive and tell people why you can't pay and when you expect to be able to send them the money. Being honest usually wins you the time you need.

Here are just a few quick tips to help you get paid, whoever it is that owes you money:

→ Always make sure you both have a written record of what it was you agreed to do. Sometimes people don't pay because they expect you to do more.
→ Always check that your customer is satisfied before issuing your invoice.
→ Always send a short, friendly reminder just before payment is due.
→ When payment becomes overdue:

- contact regularly to find out what the problem is;
- remain polite and constructive;
- suggest payment in instalments – that way you get some;
- if nothing else, agree when you're going to ring next.

When someone really cannot or will not pay, you can take them to court to recover your debt. This can be fairly simple and successful if it's to resolve a dispute, or long and torturous if your debtors simply haven't got the money. Sometimes it's easier to write off a debt and move on than let the issue niggle you for months. The fact is that if someone simply doesn't have the money, obtaining judgement against them in court won't make them any more able to pay.

Assets and reserves – what's good and what's risky

Different kinds of organisations have different policies about holding assets and maintaining reserves. Acquiring assets, particularly buildings, means taking on debt; something many charities are reluctant to do. Equally, it is considered good practice for a charity to hold in reserves perhaps 25–50% of its annual turnover, to cover the cost of winding the organisation up if funding should cease.

A commercial company, on the other hand, will probably take on lots of debt as it needs investment to deliver the eventual profit. It will also have no money in reserve and likely as not, use an overdraft to fund it through the month.

Neither approach is right or wrong, but they are very different. In fact there are often also significant attitudes to risk between charity and commerce. Many charity Boards will be nervous if they can't see the next six month's funding committed from their customers. Conversely, a pub will open its door in the morning with no guarantee that people will come in and buy food or beer.

As a social entrepreneur, you will be dealing with people from both ends of the risk spectrum. You need to recognise the cultural differences between them and choose where along that spectrum your own organisation or project needs to be. If you're too cautious, you won't get off the ground. If you're too rash, the more conservative funder will not want to support you.

Striking the balance as a social entrepreneur

Charity	Social Enterprise	Commercial business
Maintains free reserves of 25–50% of annual income	Most of profit retained and modest 'rainy day' reserves	Profits distributed and limited cash retained

What works

Understand the cultural difference between charity and business when deciding how much risk your enterprise is going to take. Not everyone will agree with what you decide, but what you decide will be what is right for you.

In summary

🐣 Like it or not, a healthy cash flow is vital to any organisation.

🐣 Keep track of what you're owed or risk running short of cash.

🐣 Decide and agree who you will pay promptly and who might wait.

🐣 If you set budgets, however small, your expenditure will be more planned.

🐣 Sustainability and respect are won through firm but fair pricing and cost recovery.

🐣 Even things you do for nothing should be costed.

🐣 Set your prices according to what people will pay, not what things cost.

🐣 Be firm and fair with people who owe you money, and persistent.

🐣 Charities and commerce have almost opposing views on financial risk. Social entrepreneurs have to find their own middle path between the extremes.

Find out more

Wayland Radio   waylandradio.com

13

Being Different, Looking Different

'Nice to see you – to see you nice.'
Bruce Forsyth, *The Generation Game*, from 1973

Branding in a nutshell

It is human nature to want to be liked. It is also true to say that nobody can be universally popular. We all get on best with the people with whom we have most in common. When you first meet someone, your conversation inevitably starts with finding the common ground. Who do you both know? What work do you do? Which football team do you support? What is your favourite fashion brand?

The way you dress and wear your hair, together with the car you drive (if you have one) and the places you choose to hang out, all signal to others the kind of person you are. Stiletto heels, red fishnet stockings and a very revealing dress, say one thing, whereas flat shoes, a tweed skirt and pearl necklace say another.

The way you present yourself to the world becomes your personal brand. It enables people to make assumptions about you that you hope are correct. It means that in a crowded room, you will choose to approach and introduce yourself to someone you feel is more likely to share your values, interests and aspirations.

It's no different for an organisation. It will be more visible and attractive to the right people if it projects its values and purpose in a clear and obvious way. The way you define this for your organisation could be summarised as its brand.

The large corporate marketers invest vast sums in developing and promoting major brands. They do this by developing a strong brand personality, brand values and words, logos and straplines that make their brand visible and appealing to their target audience.

Exercise

Think about your favourite brand of soft drink. In your mind's eye you will instantly see:

- the product name and perhaps the place you usually buy it;
- the logo and the way the product is packaged;
- advertising slogans or campaigns you particularly liked and remember;
- happy times you might have had whilst consuming the drink.

Think now about what that drink costs to make and the price you pay in the shop. It's likely that the production costs are low and the market price high. Perhaps half of the price is needed to cover the marketing costs. That's because the only way to add value to the product is by brand development.

As a social entrepreneur, your actions, mission and values can speak loudly on your behalf. This means that you can achieve a high level of brand awareness and brand understanding at modest cost. In your favour is the fact that most people, if all else is equal, will prefer to deal with a social enterprise than a business out simply to make profit for its shareholders.

To brand your organisation

However, to gain the maximum effect you do need to clearly brand what you do. You can do this most cost effectively by:

→ naming your organisation and your products and services in ways that make it clear what it is you do;

→ developing a strapline that you use at every opportunity;

→ using metaphor and perhaps even humour to make these memorable;

→ having a visual identity that is clear, simple and explicit.

Imagine that you are a health service podiatrist. You accept the challenge to create a social enterprise and subsidise your work with some fee paying clients. You also have to compete now for your funded clients who can choose where to go.

You need to brand your clinic and its work to be clearly a social enterprise, trading to protect and enhance local services. You might decide to call your clinic 'Quickstep' as you can see paying clients at short notice. You can then build on this to explain that profits from fee paying private work funds otherwise unavailable treatments for perhaps the elderly.

What works

The more authentic and genuine your mission, the more readily others will see it. Make wearing your heart on your sleeve part of your organisation's brand.

Why people prefer social enterprises

Logic says that given the choice, most people would prefer to trade with a business that has a strong social or environmental purpose. However, human behaviour is not driven by logic but by emotion. Most people choose the option that makes them feel good, rather than the one that does good. Your challenge is to combine the two.

If you return to those six buying motives, summarised by the mnemonic SPACED and add some likely caveats, you might create a list like this:

SPACED	Customer thinks	But also decides
Security	You're saving the planet	I'm not going to pay any extra
Performance	I'm keen to help the less able	I don't expect less of a service
Appearance	I want to be seen to support	I'll look silly if you let me down
Convenience	You're local, that's good	I don't have time to deal with any mistakes you might make
Economy	Gosh, you are cheap	Perhaps too cheap? Why?
Durability	You're subsidised right?	So does this mean you might disappear at short notice?

You can see that for every positive reason for dealing with you as a social entrepreneur, there is also a nagging concern. Your challenge is to recognise that your customers might have similar concerns and deal with them one by one.

Let's take a look at the different kinds of customer you might have. Why might they choose to support you and what might also hold them back?

Consumers

Stop someone at random on the street, buy them a coffee and have a conversation. You'll find as likely as not that they are essentially good, honest, responsible and caring. Most people are, providing you treat them with respect and dignity.

It is also true to say that most people complete their journey from cradle to grave without doing anything remarkable or ambitious. They simply live their lives modestly, in the company of family, friends, neighbours and workmates. They have views, sometimes strong ones, about social and environmental issues. Unlike you, they do not feel motivated, or have the opportunity, to act in as significant way as you can as a social entrepreneur.

Your opportunity with the public at large is to give them the chance to make a difference. You do this by enabling them to buy products and services they need or perhaps simply want. In other words, they may not want to dramatically change their lives, but they can change lives without much effort if they choose to support your venture.

What works

If you sell to the general public, use the opportunity to bring to life for them even the most modest contribution they may choose to make to your cause. Be their opportunity to change the world, in ways they can value.

Consumers will buy from social enterprises because:

→ they feel the venture belongs to them, for example a community shop;
→ it meets an existing or perceived need in a new and interesting way;
→ the cost is no higher and the quality no lower than the alternatives;

➡ it's considered cool amongst their peer group to be supporting a social enterprise.

Great Ryburgh Village Shop, Norfolk – With support from the Plunkett Foundation and local Community Rural Council, villagers purchased their village shop. Set up as a CIC, the store is popular with the local community because they know it is their shop. Profits are used to improve the shop and widen the range of services it provides.

Businesses

Every commercial venture is managed by people. Somehow though, people running commercial ventures distance themselves from their human nature and behave in a 'corporate' way. That is, they suppress the emotional decision-making process and instead rely on logic to make what they feel are the right choices.

This behaviour can make businesses, particularly big businesses, behave in what can seem quite inhuman ways, favouring profit over people and often planet too. Fortunately most businesses in the world are small and owner managed.

UK Businesses

➡ 3.5m self-employed people working for themselves;
➡ 1m employing 1–9 people;
➡ 170k employing 10–49 people;
➡ 27k employing 50–249 people;
➡ 6k employing more than 250 people.

What works

There are few large companies and all have established CSR policies and practices. Focus your effort on the smaller ones for whom supporting you gives them the same CSR benefits their bigger rivals enjoy.

Your opportunity with the many smaller businesses and self-employed people is to enable them to do the things they cannot afford to do for themselves.

Businesses will buy from social enterprises because:

→ they want to demonstrate their commitment in a way that will enhance their own reputation;
→ it adds value to what they are already doing;
→ there is no financial penalty;
→ it can generate them positive publicity and so form part of their marketing.

Break, Norfolk – Break is a trading charity that helps people with disabilities and long-term mental health difficulties. It runs a network of charity shops that together contribute more than £2m of income annually.

In 1985, long before most big businesses were linking with social enterprises, Break linked up with Rowntree Mackintosh who ran a promotion linking Break to their Kit Kat bar. The advertising slogan 'Have a break, have a Kit Kat' lent itself to a joint promotion. Lots of Kit Kats were purchased and Break were given £300000 which they used to build swimming pools at their holiday centres.

Public sector

An increasing number of social enterprises are emerging from the public sector. Others, such as Housing Associations and many quangos, have public sector roots. All have much in common and can largely be considered to behave in a similar way.

Public sector organisations are in general committed to supporting social enterprise. They are also risk averse and protect themselves with complicated tendering and contracting procedures. These are meant to give equal opportunity to all but their complexity can often deter the smaller organisations from pitching for work.

Your opportunity is to partner with public sector organisations in ways that help them fulfil their own social and environmental goals. Many social entrepreneurs choose to do this by getting to know people within these organisations and taking the time and trouble to understand their aspirations.

What works

Working with the public sector is often best achieved by understanding what their social aims are and then translating your offer into the outputs you know they will value.

Public sector organisations will buy from social enterprises because:

→ it clearly provides them with the social impact/outcomes they want to see;
→ they can see little risk in working with your organisation;
→ you have developed the ability to speak their language;

➡ those elected from the community to govern them want to be inclusive.

> **Cornwall Council** spends around £450m a year and has some 20,000 suppliers. The Council positively encourage bids from social enterprises and from voluntary and community organisations. In common with all public sector bodies it tries hard to do business with local organisations that actively work towards improving the lives and prospects of disadvantaged people.

Practical ways to look professional

In the past, too many campaigners and activists seeking social or environmental change were radical in their approach. They were prepared to make large sacrifices to deliver rapid change and encouraged others to do the same. This won them few followers because most people do not want to become martyrs to any cause.

People today tend to be innately suspicious of anything that promises to deliver extraordinary results. They have seen those who make bold claims come and go and know deep down that sustainable change only results from repeated short steps in the right direction.

Personally, you might be a real firebrand, eager to challenge then change the world quickly. To win support, you need to temper your passion with the practical. That way people will more readily relate to what you are trying to do and see how they can share and subscribe to your vision.

Tradition dictates that enterprise should be focused solely on profit. To successfully introduce social and environmental goals to your customers, you need to project a very professional image. So too does your organisation. In fact because people might question the viability of a social enterprise over for profit alone enterprises, you have to work harder at being seen to be professional.

Personal professionalism

How you look will largely dictate the first impression you make on others. That's not to say you need to wear formal business attire. Instead you need to work on your personal image and make sure it projects the right messages about you and your work. In fact for many business areas, there are almost 'uniforms' that most people wear. For example:

- Financial services – people wear dark formal suits to suggest they know what they're talking about.
- Retail – uniforms, so that customers can find a staff member easily.
- Travel – formal uniforms, especially airline pilots, to boost passenger confidence.

Depending on the sector you work in, you might choose a uniform for your people. You might also choose to wear the same yourself, even when going out to meet new customers. It can after all suggest that you firmly believe in equality and do not want to put yourself apart from your team or even service users.

Alternatively, you can dress in a way that is very individual and clearly differentiates you from others in your marketplace. If you do this, remember it's good to be individual but not too 'off the wall'. You will need to do business with people who might be put off by too much flamboyance.

Organisational professionalism

Just as you have to look the part, so does your enterprise have to deliver the promise. People can be quick to dismiss and you need to work extra hard to make sure your social enterprise is as professional as it can be in its presentation.

For example, a mental health charity providing 'back to work' training and work experience might not be best represented by putting its less able service users on the switchboard. Of course they need to show that they are inclusive and promote equality in every aspect of their work, but pragmatism says that the swift and efficient fielding of incoming calls is perhaps more important than making a point.

To project a professional image as an organisation you might consider:

➡ staff uniforms if you work in a retail environment;
➡ staff training so that all customer/client facing people get it right;
➡ written service standards, so that everyone knows what is expected;
➡ professionally prepared promotional materials;
➡ publishing testimonials so people can see how you meet customer/client needs and expectations.

What works

Not only do you have to be professional, you have to look professional too. You only have one chance to make a good first impression.

The Social Enterprise Mark

Quality marks and professional memberships have long been used as quick and convenient ways to demonstrate values and abilities. Look at the letterhead of almost any organisation and you see the logos of the different bodies they belong to, each policing a particular aspect of each member's performance.

Individuals often demonstrate their knowledge and skills by adding the relevant letters after their name on business cards and the like.

In the UK, the Social Enterprise Mark was launched in 2010 to provide social enterprises with a very clear way to demonstrate they met a common standard. The logo is increasingly appearing on literature, advertising and even in signage outside the premises of social enterprises that have been successfully assessed against the Social Enterprise Mark standard.

In short, the Mark is only awarded to organisations that work primarily for social or environmental purposes. To qualify, they have to reinvest at least 50% of their profits in those social or environmental goals. Universally accepted by sector leaders and Government, acquiring the Mark is a very convenient and visible way of showing the world that you are running a social enterprise.

Even if you choose not to seek formal recognition of your status as a social enterprise, the qualification criteria for the Social Enterprise Mark are worth embracing. In fact they form a useful checklist in themselves for the extent to which others might regard your enterprise a social enterprise.

Social Enterprise Mark qualification criteria

➡ Have social/environmental objectives written into your constitutional documents.

➡ Be clearly an independent, self governing organization.

➡ Earn more than 50% of your income from trading.

➡ Invest at least 50% of your profits in your social/environmental objectives.

➡ Have written into your constitutional documents that when the enterprise is dissolved, residual assets will be distributed for social/environmental purposes.

➡ Demonstrate that you are already making a difference and that you commit to uphold the standards expected of Mark holders.

As with all quality criteria, once achieved it is important to maintain the standard in every aspect of the organisation's work. No standard is a guarantee of performance, so as with any other, it pays to check out the fit between your values and those of any organisation you choose to deal with.

In a sector such as social enterprise that is rapidly taking shape and growing, it will make good sense for many social enterprises to benchmark themselves against a widely recognised standard by gaining the Social Enterprise Mark.

Today the UK, tomorrow the world

The Social Enterprise Mark launched in the UK early in 2010. Already the model is being piloted in other countries, each eager to follow the success seen in the UK. Check out their website to find out what other countries the Mark is going to be introduced to.

In summary

C People will only support a social enterprise when its offer matches that of their usual, commercial supplier.

C Most businesses are small and so base business decisions as much on emotion as logic.

C You and your organisation need to look professional if you are to be taken seriously.

C The Social Enterprise Mark is a convenient, off the shelf way to show the world you are a social enterprise.

Find out more

UK business statistics – Department for Business Innovation and Skills	http://stats.bis.gov.uk/ed/sme
International Federation of Image Consultants	tfic.org.uk
The Social Enterprise Mark	socialenterprisemark.org.uk

Part Five
How to Share

14

Effective Communication

'Think like a wise man but communicate in the language of the people.'
W B Yeats, 1865–1939

Saying it like it is

The paradox of communication is that although people talk all the time, what they are saying is frequently not heard. People in long-term relationships often accuse their partner of 'selective hearing'. They are right, but not as they suspect because the partner is not listening. It is because once our brain has picked up enough of what it is hearing to make an assumption about what comes next, it does so automatically. In other words, what we hear is often translated automatically into what our brains think was said.

The same applies to written information too. We scan text and make assumptions about what each word is based on, its shape and position relative to other words we recognise more readily.

As an entrepreneur, you are in the business of introducing new concepts, ideas and opportunities to people. To do this you have to communicate clearly and effectively and check constantly that those reading or hearing you understand. It's how conversation works, with each participant correcting the other as they develop the strand of common thought.

However, you communicate as a social entrepreneur, it is vital that you do so clearly, effectively and with frequent checks to make sure you are being heard correctly. Now let's look at who you must communicate with and how you can influence them most effectively.

Customer recruitment

As you will remember, customers are the people who pay you for what you do. Clients are those who use the products or services you provide. The difference is important as without one you cannot have the other. To complicate things, customers can be clients too, perhaps buying for their own use.

Your drive as a social entrepreneur needs to be focused equally on both customers and clients. Customers fund your business, so they need to be recruited first.

Let's look at three quite different customer groups and how you might go about recruiting each.

Funders

Finding funders is for many in the charity world a full-time occupation. Because you are selling your funders something, rather than shaking a metaphorical tin under their noses, you need to be more selective and less brazen. Whilst fundraising is about flattery, finding funders to invest in your venture is a more subtle, selective process.

First you have to work out what you want and why. Only when you have worked out what value supporting you provides your funder, can you go in search of one. Funders are buying measurable outputs. For example:

Funder	Will pay for	Start your search here
Statutory agency	Outputs linked to recognised social/ environmental problems (e.g. unemployment, climate change).	Read national, regional and local strategy documents that name agencies, their goals and their budgets.
Winners of major contracts	Local delivery of outputs by well connected, reliable sub-contractors.	Winners of major tenders are published on statutory agency websites.

Recruiting from these groups demands a process of careful research. Fortunately publicly paid for projects are easy to find via:

→ tender invitations on public body websites;
→ contracts awarded lists that you can match with the tender to see what the winner has to deliver.

Having identified your target funder, you have to build rapport with the key people who influence where work is placed. Whilst the actual tender process will be scrupulously open and fair, it is important to be known by at least some of those who will make the decision.

You will be more successful at recruiting funders if you can demonstrate that you:

→ have proven experience of working with the target client group;
→ are professional and businesslike, rather than a passionate campaigner;
→ can illustrate your abilities with robust case studies.

What works

The best time to get to know people in public sector funding organisations is before they issue a tender you wish to bid for. You may find that once a tender has been issued they will not be able to talk to you in case this is construed as favouring you as a bidder.

Businesses

You will rarely find a business tendering for a partner to deliver social outcomes. Instead you will need to introduce the idea that working with your social enterprise can help them. Good ways to do this include:

→ Approaching competitors of businesses already partnering with a charity or social enterprise to show how you can help them do the same:
  • they will be aware of the opportunity;
  • you have something to compare your offer against.
→ Identifying businesses with whom you have some overlap of mission:
  • they might link your organisation to a product promotion;
  • their staff could volunteer with your organisation;
  • you might stock and sell their products and enjoy a better deal than you might otherwise enjoy.

For example:

→ A local newspaper could sponsor your community woodland, demonstrating commitment to both local readers and sustainable timber use.
→ A supermarket could pledge to always have a number of your trainees on work experience. This both delivers you outcomes for which your public sector funder pays, but also enables the supermarket to gain valuable local publicity as customers learn of the relationship.
→ A restaurant could buy produce from your gardening project and create some special dishes that promote the relationship.

In each of these three examples, you have the added opportunity of publicising and promoting your organisation to the customers of each business. That's because they could themselves become your customers.

Private service users

Imagine you are going on holiday and need to book a hotel. Depending on your budget, past experience and aspiration, you may choose to stay in a luxury five star place with soft fluffy towels and 24hr room service. On the other hand, you might simply want somewhere cheap and basic to rest between bouts of sunbathing and dancing the night away in the beach-front disco.

Neither choice is better than the other, but both are very different. If you habitually chose the luxury option you might be doubtful if offered a 'luxury package' by the nearby back-packers' hostel.

It's the same feeling a city banker might feel when in search of a drug detox he or she stumbles upon a charity that works with homeless drug addicts offering 'private clients' a high quality deal. You'd not be surprised if the banker doubted the organisation's ability to offer a quality experience. Then there's the embarrassment of meeting service users from the street in the waiting room.

That said, private service users can and do offer valuable revenue that can subsidise or even fund similar work with the disadvantaged. The biggest challenge is reassuring those who see your marketing message that you really can offer two levels of service.

You can attract private service users who pay for their support by:

➡ having two very different premises for service users to visit. At least you need two front doors and two sets of client consulting rooms;

→ inviting professionals who might recommend you (senior corporate HR folk and health advisers) to visit and see for themselves what you can offer;

→ collecting case studies and testimonials (albeit they will need to be anonymous).

What works

Private service users provide a great opportunity. Your biggest challenge is not finding them; it's clearly demonstrating you can adapt to meet the higher expectations of a more discerning client group.

Retail customers

As with private service users, retail customers of all kinds need to know that you are competent and professional in everything you do. For example, if you and your neighbours have just saved your village pub from closure, people will want to know that you know how to keep beer and serve tasty food. In other words, the experience has to very different from say going to a party at a friend's house.

With any retail project, be it a shop, a smallholding or furniture project, it's the first impression that makes all the difference. You need to look at how successful private sector outlets present themselves and then do the same.

Success in any retail business is largely dictated by location. If you're in the right place, enough people will pass your door. If they like what they see, they'll come in. If what you offer excites them, they'll buy. It's both that simple and that complicated.

The 'sanctuary or zoo' debate

People running retail social enterprises that also provide employment and training opportunities frequently wrestle with this debate. The question they ask themselves is this: 'do we make our service user staff a point of difference or do we ignore the fact that we're a social enterprise and succeed on merit alone?'

The worry is always that by drawing attention to your service users and their additional needs, you create a zoo. The alternative is to protect them from customers and create a sanctuary.

What seems to work best is to strike a happy balance between the two. That means you can be honest with your customers about why you're in business and honest with your staff about sensitively highlighting their differences in your marketing.

What works

If everybody in a social enterprise wears the same type of clothes, or even a company uniform, no one can tell who's on the payroll and who is a service user.

Client recruitment

If you are being funded at least in part with public money you'll have output targets to hit. These will be defined in your contract and may well be more closely related to funder vision than the reality of your day to day work.

The client recruitment challenge can often be compounded by your funder's desire to impose strict demographic targets. In other words, the right mix of age, employment status, ethnic origin and level of qualification. It can make finding clients difficult as the hardest to reach groups are, not surprisingly, hard to reach!

You cannot assume that just because you're offering them something free, your service users will be queuing at the door. Sometimes they do not respond for the very reason that the offer is free and therefore is seen to be of little value.

When recruiting clients make sure you:

→ highlight the benefit to the service user, including those your funder might not value or recognise, but your research shows to be valued;
→ ask them to make a tangible commitment, in kind if not in cash, so that they have an incentive to actually turn up;
→ add to the programme something they will enjoy, even if it's free food.

As well as all the usual marketing materials (see next section) you will find the following useful ways to recruit clients:

→ Via existing, informal networks that exist with the communities your project is targeting. Get the community leaders on your side and let them 'own' elements of the project.
→ Word of mouth, where satisfied service users, their family and professional carers/advisers spread the word.
→ Go where the people already can be found. In other words, if your target audience hang out in the park, or use a particular pub, take the trouble to go there and talk to people.

What works

Make your starting point what's there, not what you'd like to create. Remember that it's often easier to go to the people than to persuade the people to come to you.

Online and offline promotion

The rapid growth in internet usage, particularly via mobile telephones, has transformed the way we choose to receive and retain information. Of course there is a generational lag and older people still prefer to pick up a leaflet at the library or doctors. Most of working age and all of the young are as likely to search online.

Websites

Your most significant promotional piece is your website. You probably already have a website but is it working hard enough for you? Increasingly anybody wanting to find out about your organisation is going to look at your website. It is certainly where people will go to check out your credentials and see evidence of your commitment to delivering that triple bottom line (profit, people and planet).

The first glance

Your home page and the top level pages that lead from it are really important. The who, what, why, when, where and how of what you do needs to be clear and immediately obvious. These are the first pages visitors see and so they need to be:

➡ **Factual** explaining in as few words as possible exactly what your organisation is about.

➡ **Frank** and objective, saying what you do without hype or gushing enthusiasm.

➡ **Full** enough to answer the most basic questions the viewer will have in their mind. As a social entrepreneur you might choose to include your social or environmental goals where they are easy to find.

Looking further

Once you have captured your visitor's interest, you need to feed them information that:

➡ **Explains** what you do in sufficient detail for them to want to contact you to find out what you can do for them.

➡ **Shares** enough of your governance and financial data to reassure that you are above board and viable. If you are a CIC it could be good to publish the form on which you describe your 'community of interest'. You might also consider publishing an extract from your accounts on your website.

➡ **Invites** people to get in touch, for information, case studies, to arrange a visit, to receive regular e-newsletters etc. The more choice you offer, the more likely it is that people will get in touch.

Finally are some additional tips that might help you make it more useful:

➡ **Content management** – it's vital you have the ability and make the time to keep your website up to date. Freshly added content and out of date stuff taken down is vital. If your website is out of date, people will assume you are too.

➡ **Live links** – you need to lots of links in to your site from other places. However, these need to be relevant places, so blog, comment on blogs and encourage your funders and business associates to create links to your website.

➡ **RSS** – enables people to automatically receive a notification whenever any new content is added.

➡ **Simplicity** – good websites are simple. Easy to navigate, easy to understand and easy to read, even for those with poor eyesight.

For inspiration look at how other similar organisations present themselves online. See how easy it is to find out all you think a customer or client might want to know. This will give you ideas you can use on your own website.

Also, look at other sites, unrelated to your business sector. They can teach you a lot and inspire you too. For example:

➡ **Newspaper** websites are excellent at arranging and presenting a lot of information in a simple and navigable way.

➡ **Think tank** websites are often very good presenting opinion and research, then managing online debate and comment. Useful if you want to enable people to interact on your website.

➡ **Online communities** such as www.businesszone.co.uk also present a lot of information in a very clear way. They also enable people to join and contribute content.

What works

It is usually more effective to keep your website relevant and up to date than to spend money on someone working to raise your search engine rankings.

Print

If your organisation produces printed materials it's important that they are concise, explicit and focus on what you do, not what you are. If you have a number of different customer or client groups, it is usually better to summarise all that you offer in one document than produce a suite. That's because:

→ you can never quite predict who will be interested in what;
→ you want to encourage people to pass your literature on to others;
→ it's almost always cheaper to produce one, all embracing profile than a myriad of small leaflets.

If you're not familiar with buying print it can be confusing. Many printers will also design materials for you. You might also have a budding creative in your team who is handy with Microsoft Publisher™.

However, more often than not, your best option is to find a young enthusiastic graphic designer. Choose one who buys into your ideals and has recently started out. Give them the opportunity to:

→ help you see your organisation in a new, perhaps different way;
→ suggest creative ways to share your mission and message;
→ provide you with professional literature.

Print also adds a third dimension to your promotional activity. It is physical, tactile and has weight. You can introduce texture and shape too, within the limitations of what is practical and affordable. A good tip is to temper your enthusiasm for recycled paper and instead use paper from sustainable sources. This subtle difference will save you money without compromising your environmental credentials.

Lastly a few points about what to put in your promotional print:

→ Professional photography is almost always worth the investment, bringing your work to life and adding real reader appeal.

→ Packages or bundled services will make more sense than a long list. Brand each package, or use the tried and trusted 'gold, silver or bronze' levels to differentiate the best from the standard.

→ Don't say too much in your promotional literature. Just enough to prompt the reader to contact you.

→ Sometimes, a well-designed single colour brochure can be more striking and powerfull at a lower cost than full colour, colour isn't everything!

What works

Just as they say people judge a book by its cover, so too will they judge your organisation by its print. Fewer good quality pieces will always achieve more than many poor quality leaflets.

Language

Every industry has its own language, jargon and acronyms. Even if you think everyone you deal with speaks the same language, avoid industry-speak at all costs. As a social entrepreneur you cannot make any assumptions about who will read your promotional messages and how they will interpret them.

Whatever you write remember that:

→ writing it as you would say it makes text easier to read and understand;

➝ if you need to look a word up, it's the wrong word. Use
  one we all know;
➝ today's buzzword is tomorrow's cliché;
➝ avoid euphemisms and say it like it is;
➝ the fewer words you use, the stronger the message;
➝ pictures save words so use lots of pictures.

A new manager took over a community café on an estate
where many migrant workers lived. Many came to the door,
looked in and then went away. Puzzled, he asked a few what
the problem was; that they were not confident enough as
English speakers to walk in and place an order.

The manager thought for a while and then photographed
an example of every dish on the menu when it was next prepared. The photos were then printed out and pinned to the
wall beside the counter, in full view of the door.

Soon new people started coming in. Many ordered by
pointing and soon the ice was broken. The manager could
have printed multilingual menu cards, but actually the photos
worked better and cost a lot less too.

Getting the press to cover your news

News coverage is potentially your cheapest and by far most
effective marketing tool. Being featured in your local paper,
the social enterprise press or even appearing on TV can literally
make millions aware of your work. What's more it can achieve
this at no cost to you, apart from a little time and planning.

The media

The recent recession hit the media hard. Falling advertising
revenues has meant a reduction in the number of journalists

searching out news stories. There is also a rise in popularity of reality TV shows, where people from all walks of life have the chance to pitch for funding, enjoy a business makeover and much more.

Most publications, particularly the trade and local press are therefore usually quite keen to hear from people with a good story to share. All you have to do is tell them in a way they'll find appealing.

Good stories

The key point to remember is that what you might consider a good story might not resonate quite so loudly with readers of the titles you approach. They will see your organisation quite differently from you. What they find interesting will also be different. Good stories are those with:

- a direct connection to the reader, local and relevant to them;
- novelty, in that it's something new and different;
- currency and of the moment, not something that happened months ago;
- connection with bigger, global or national issues.

Examples of good stories might be:

- a major contract win in which you can say how much money and how many jobs have been created (or saved);
- human interest stories about how service users have made huge progress with your help and support, say getting a job or losing weight;
- significant environmental achievements that support your cause, for example the discovery of rare orchids on a recently established nature reserve.

Pictures

A good photograph with a 20-word caption can often have more impact on the page than a 500 word article. Press photographs need:

→ to feature people;
→ not too much branding, i.e. your signage;
→ to be unusual, perhaps the juxtaposition of two familiar things in a visual way (for example, a comfy bed under a flyover to illustrate that you're now able to offer more beds to homeless people).

Making your approach

It's usually more effective to make a direct approach to the right journalist by email before sending in what you think they might find interesting. This means you only write something that's wanted and they are spared at least some of the flood of news releases that usually can be quickly discarded.

The best way to approach the media is:

→ Identify and read the output of the journalists who seem to write most frequently about the issues, sector or place you are involved with.
→ When you have an idea for a story, email them a very, very brief synopsis in the body of an email. Mention how it links with something you know they covered earlier.
→ Follow up with a second email asking for feedback if you don't hear anything within a few days.
→ Once you have their interest, talk to them on the phone and find out:
   • what angle they think would make the story most interesting;

- if they want to visit, or do a phone interview, or have
  you write the story in outline for them to edit;
- when their deadline is;

➡ Always suggest photos and if you can, send a low
resolution image in your email for their reference. Offer
to commission a photographer as this will be your
only cost.

➡ Deliver what you promise ahead of the deadline.

Finding publications

There are a number of websites that list publications. www.
mediauk.com, for example, is searchable so you can find titles
you've not heard of. Major publishing groups such as www.
ipcmedia.com list all of their titles, as well as sites for each
publication.

Exercise

Search 'Google News' using a phrase that summarises your
story (for example, 'social enterprise contract win') to see who
has recently written similar stories. Then you can email the
journalist and explain how your story links to the one they've
recently published.

News release

Sometimes though, you need to send a news release. For
the national press and if you feel you need to contact a lot
of journalists quickly, it is the only way. There are a few

simple rules for news releases which are, from the top of the page:

→ Add today's date and the date after which it can be published.
→ Make the headline summarise the story in one line.
→ The first paragraph contains the key points.
→ The second contains a quote, which needs to be short and specific as if used it will be used in its entirety.
→ The third gives vital supporting information such as how to get in touch with you.
→ Further paragraphs can be added – or you can simply say that more is available on request.
→ Give a name and phone number for them to follow up. Include a mobile number for out of hours calls (journalists often work strange hours).
→ Finally, add a 'boilerplate'. This is a paragraph that literally summarises the organisation, it's age, size, role etc.
→ If you attach photos, number the JPEG file and add captions on the bottom of the news release.
→ If you have photographed children or vulnerable adults, confirm that you have the necessary permissions for them to be published.

What works

Daily papers are always hungry for news to fill Monday's paper. As a rule, a marginal story has a better chance of success if sent in on a Thursday or Friday than on a Monday or Tuesday. That's because Monday's paper is often largely written at the end of the preceding week.

In summary

🐣 You need to look for customers before clients as these are the people who will pay you for what you do.

🐣 It can sometimes be better to sub-contract to a tender winner and only do what you do well, than to win the whole tender and struggle.

🐣 Just as trains have First Class carriages so too can you enable people to enjoy different levels of service at different prices, but sharing the same basic experience.

🐣 Retail success is all about detail and location – whatever your venture.

🐣 If you believe in equality, wear the same clothes as your service users and do not make your suit and tie (or similar) set you apart from those you are there to support.

🐣 For a surprisingly large number of your customers and clients, their first port of call will be your website.

🐣 Promote your enterprise using simple language, clear messages and professional print.

🐣 News coverage is free, but you need to focused, timely and sometimes quite creative.

Find out more

UK public contract tender alerts   supply2.gov.uk

15

Building a Winning Team

'Is my team ploughing,
That I used to drive,
And hear the harness jingle,
When I was man alive.'
A E Houseman, *A Shropshire Lad,* 1896

The evolving organisation – when to recruit

A business established just to make money only really becomes valuable when it can continue to grow without its founder making all the decisions. When the owner can step back confident the tills will keep jingling, it's time to sell and start again.

Social entrepreneurs, however visionary and passionate, cannot change the world alone. They need others to help them. In the early stages these could simply be friends and acquaintances lending a hand. As your organisation develops you will need more organised and planned assistance. That's when you start to hire people and recruit volunteers.

Eventually, it will be time for you to move on from the organisations you've established. Right now this might seem impossible to imagine, but given time and success, your organisation will evolve and take on a life of its own. It will need different skills to manage and lead it at each stage of its life. This is true even if the organisation will never be sold because it provides a valuable community service that will always be needed.

In fact it could be argued that whilst social entrepreneurs are often great at starting social enterprises, they may often be the wrong people to lead them long term. The pioneering spirit you need at the outset differs markedly from the organisational talents you need to keep the growing enterprise on track.

How enterprises grow

Most new enterprises are the brainchild of one person. They either start the enterprise from scratch, or lead it as a trading offshoot of another already established organisation. Both are defined by their autonomy and individuality.

These are the stages of growth most organisations experience:

1. **Pioneer** – everything is new and driven by opportunity, fuelled by hard work and managed informally. You 'fly by the seat of your pants'.
2. **Settler** – you've found what works for you and settled in a particular market niche. You expand what you do to strengthen your market hold.
3. **Builder** – things get bigger and more complex, you have to let go and delegate. The founder is now the builder, but no longer in the front line.
4. **Bureaucrat** – further growth means costs and risks are higher, but then so are the opportunities. It becomes important to measure things and systems emerge.
5. **Rebel** – the organisation has reached its peak in terms of size and scope. Merger, acquisition, partnerships is the way ahead. The few who remain from the early stages leave to do their own thing. They start again.

Not all organisations make it through each stage. This is in part because of the environment in which they find themselves; situations change and some adapt better than others. More often than not, it's the founder's inability to grow, delegate and manage that causes an organisation to peak before reaching its full potential. That's why as a social entrepreneur it's important to get the right people, with the right skills, to help you grow your organisation.

What works

All organisations outgrow people as they grow. Create a structure and culture where it's OK to move on if you feel out of your depth. That applies as much to the founder as to the team.

What to recruit

As a social entrepreneur, you are probably more willing than most to accept that your organisation needs to grow and reach its full potential. Most 'for profit only' entrepreneurs cap growth once they can see the income coming in regularly. To grow further means developing themselves and not everyone wants to do that.

You, though, are driven more by the need to deliver social or environmental change and usually that hunger is harder to sate than your personal wealth aspirations. This means you will recruit people and grow your organisation.

You need different people at each stage of your organisation's growth. For example:

Stage	People to look for
Pioneer	Passionate, enthusiastic and able people like yourself
	Skilled front line staff capable of working on their own initiative
	People who like informality, freedom and are 'low maintenance'
Settler	People with knowledge, networks and experience in your sector
	Support skills such as finance and marketing
	People eager to develop their skills and grow with the organisation
Builder	Professional managers, perhaps looking for a job with real purpose
	People able to manage key customer relationships
	Newcomers to the sector, that you can train and develop

Stage	People to look for
Bureaucrat	Senior managers and perhaps a non executive Board
	Systems and processes
	HR and IT support
Rebel	Innovators and ideas people, to help define future opportunity
	A CEO to enable you to move on yourself

Who to recruit

You don't have to take on everyone you need as an employee. You can use volunteers, freelancers, interns, agency staff and consultants. Even those you do hire can be on a flexible contract so you only have them when you need them.

Commitment though is a two-way street. The more the organisation commits to an individual, the more that individual will commit to the organisation. This is important when you grow an organisation as it is almost impossible to match workload with staffing levels. That's why the people you hire in the early days will be different from those who will join an established organisation later.

Here are some pros and cons to the different types of people you could recruit:

	Positive points	Potential problems
Volunteers	Cost very little	Difficult to manage
	Can bring otherwise unaffordable skills	May be unreliable
Interns	Modest cost	New to the workplace
	Project focused	May be inflexible if needs change

	Positive points	**Potential problems**
Agency staff	There when you need them	Cost more than equivalent employee
	No complicated HR issues	Might get someone different every time
Consultants	Bring expensive skills	Need clear terms of reference
	Bring useful experience	Can over-promise
Employees	Continuity and consistency	Matching workload to staffing
		An inflexible overhead cost

Defining roles and finding people

When you visit the optician you know exactly what you're paying for. He or she is going to test your eyes and give you a written report, perhaps in the form of a prescription. But when you hire someone to help in your organisation, are you as clear in your mind what it is you are looking for? Many are not and therefore should not be surprised if the resulting appointment does not work out. It doesn't matter what you need someone to do, you should always try as hard as you can to define the role and the specification of the person you think you need.

This is even true if you are hiring a consultant to solve a problem you've been grappling with for a while. Although you perhaps have yet to identify the root of the issue or consider any solutions, you will know what you want to achieve. You will also be able to define the impact you want this to have on your organisation.

What works

Most people know it's important to define what they want to happen. But sometimes you need to also define what you don't want to happen.

How to define the role

The bigger the organisation the easier this task becomes. That's because in the early stages of any organisation's life roles are of necessity fluid and flexible. But that does not mean you should not define them at all!

With any role, you need to write down as clearly and succinctly as possible what the person doing the job:

→ will be expected to do;
→ will be responsible for;
→ will be reporting to;
→ will need to know before applying;
→ will find by way of performance measurement;
→ can expect by way of reward.

It is important to do this for any role, however minor.

As your organisation grows, you will need to become more structured in how you go about this process of role definition. Not least because you may already by then have people doing similar jobs and want to plug specific expertise gaps. In other words the more sophisticated the organisation becomes, the more sophisticated the recruitment process.

Finding people

It is not unusual to visit your local convenience store and see a sign in the window advertising for staff. Buses also frequently carry ads for bus drivers. Both do this because it is quite likely that people with the right skills, looking for a job could see the ad. It's also helpful because:

→ the convenience store wants to employ people who live locally and therefore will be more likely to be able to get to work easily at any time of day or night;
→ the bus company wants drivers who notice buses and perhaps use them for their own transport. Drivers who also ride on buses will see things better from the passenger's perspective.

So the first place to look for people, be they volunteers, workers or even service users, is on your doorstep. A poster in your window is the cheapest form of advertising you can get.

Advertising

Most people look at the recruitment ads in both their local and specialist trade press. Both are good places to advertise for paid staff. But don't overlook press features or appeals for volunteers if that's what you need. A good news story that ends with an appeal for volunteers is going to cost you less than a paid for advertisement.

You can also place recruitment ads on your website and other sites you feel might be relevant. Lastly, why not put up volunteering opportunity posters on local company noticeboards, as well as other places the people you're seeking may look?

Agencies

There are two kinds of agency. Those who employ then hire out by the hour specialist staff and those who find and shortlist potential employees for a fee.

Employment agencies can provide you with hassle free cover for front line jobs. You pay more per hour than if you employed direct, but you don't have to worry about deducting tax, holiday pay or covering sick leave. Agency staff will call the agency when unable to work and they find you someone else.

Recruitment agencies can help you in many ways and are often worth the investment. For example:

→ They can advertise your job under their name, so people don't know it's you recruiting.
→ They will advertise more widely and extensively than you can because each ad carries a number of vacancies.
→ They may well already have the right person 'on their books' and not need to advertise at all.
→ They are professional recruiters and so will long list and short list more expertly.
→ They are also experienced interviewers and will pick up things you might miss.
→ If the person they find you doesn't work out, they'll usually charge you less to recruit a replacement.

What works

When worrying about paying fees to a recruitment agency, think about the value of the time you will be saving. Unless you have time to spare, DIY recruitment can often be a false economy.

Word of mouth

Never underestimate the power of word of mouth. Simply telling those you work with and around that you're looking for additional people can work wonders. People often know someone who then of course comes with some endorsement.

As your organisation grows however, you might find it increasingly difficult to rely solely on word of mouth recruitment, particularly if your customers include public sector bodies who expect to see evidence that you are an equal opportunities employer who advertises and recruits using an open and fair process.

Managing volunteers

Every organisation will experience working with volunteers, even if just local students come in to do work experience. Any business can offer volunteering opportunities, providing the benefit to the volunteer is clear and useful. As a social entrepreneur, volunteers represent a valuable resource you can use to make more of a difference in your chosen field.

People volunteer for things for a variety of reasons. These include:

- to gain useful experience that will help them get qualifications or a job;
- because they are passionate about the cause and want to help;
- to build confidence and self esteem;
- to overcome loneliness, for example following bereavement.

Whatever their personal motivation, you need to recognise that people volunteer because of what it does for them, as well as what it does for you. Only a very few organisations recognise this.

> **Preen CIC** describes itself as a 'furniture bank'. Based in Biggleswade, they collect donated furniture and household appliances which are then supplied to vulnerable and disadvantaged people. They also operate a very successful shop, popular with both collectors of classic brands and people setting up a home.
>
> Their website lists all of their staff, even the cleaner, as well as offering volunteers an interesting range of opportunities, from sharing skills, to getting fit and meeting people. What makes Preen's appeal for volunteers perhaps unique is that rather than listing what they want people to do for them, instead they list what volunteering with Preen can do for you.

Training

Volunteers need training in just the same way as your employed staff. Not only may they need input to develop their skills, but they may need to better understand why you do things the way you do. Often a volunteer will have experience that is out of date. They need to be introduced to current practice and to be encouraged to compare what you expect with what they remember.

Supervision

This can actually work both ways. Whilst you will know of course that volunteers working in your organisation need to be supervised, you might also consider recruiting volunteers able to supervise you. It is too easy to assume that volunteers are only useful for basic front line tasks. In fact very senior people in large organisations can make very effective mentors for the social entrepreneur.

What works

Find yourself a volunteer mentor who is older, wiser and further down the career path than you. This helps you to grow as well as your organisation.

Retention

As with any other team members, volunteers need to feel involved, informed and above all valued. Make sure they are kept in the loop with internal communication and reminded of the impact and value of their contribution.

Because social enterprises make money as well as a difference, volunteers need reassurance that they really are helping you make a difference, rather than simply making you money!

Recruiting other people

As well as employees and volunteers there are other people you might consider recruiting from time to time. Here are some ideas you might not have considered.

Consultants

When you need specific expertise for a short time to respond to a particular challenge or opportunity, a consultant might be the answer. Consultants come in all shapes and sizes, from large management consultancies to early retired professionals who take on ad hoc projects to supplement their pension.

When looking for a consultant:

- decide and write down exactly what you want the consultant to do;
- ask around to see who knows of people with these skills you can talk to;
- post a request on websites such as www.skillfair.co.uk where you can list your project for free and invite consultants to contact you;
- always obtain two maybe three written proposals;
- do not buy on price but track record.

Students

Students, particularly those at university, can be really useful when you have a specific project that needs to be done. You can recruit students:

- via your local university careers office who will help you find a student with the right skills seeking a part time job;
- through schemes such as www.step.org.uk that arrange and supervise summer internships;
- As post-graduate interns, again via your local university. There are a number of intern schemes around. These are sometimes academically supervised, giving you added value. Whilst your local university will act as broker, students could come from anywhere.

Mentors

As your organisation grows, you might find a mentor invaluable. This is someone who is probably older than you, knows your business sector and has probably already made the business journey you are embarking on. Additionally they might well be able to open a few doors for you, as invariably they are people with an excellent network of contacts.

You can find mentors by:

→ asking around and flattering one of the respected 'old stagers' in your sector into taking an interest in your development;

→ asking your local social enterprise network, bank, accountant or other adviser. In short anyone who knows you and is active in your sector may well be able to make an introduction.

What works

Mentors can be very effective but if you are running a limited company of any kind, you also have the option of appointing non-executive Directors. These are like mentors but sign up to share with you the legal responsibility for the company's governance and behaviour. You need to pay them a fee, but they bridge the gap well between mentor and the business partner you may not have.

Setting goals and nurturing motivation

Sales people are accustomed to being given targets to achieve and rewards for achieving them. In some business sectors, even today, this simplistic 'carrot and stick' approach to directing and motivating people remains.

Such a stark focus on financial results may not sit comfortably with your vision of social entrepreneurship. Your focus on profit and social or environmental impact is probably more balanced. Nevertheless you do need to set clear, simple, measurable goals and encourage people to work together to achieve them.

Goal setting

Your business plan provides both your own goals and the starting point for setting the goals of those who work with you. People need to be involved in setting their own goals as otherwise they will feel no sense of ownership of them.

The process of discussing and agreeing goals can involve:

→ sharing all or part of the business plan with your team;
→ asking them to identify what is possible, then discuss the gap between what is needed and what is considered possible;
→ identifying skill or training gaps that need to be plugged;
→ agreeing how performance against goals will be measured.

What works

The more people can see how they contribute to the organisation's overall success, the more motivated they are likely to be.

Team working

Return for a moment to the traditionally motivated sales team. Each member has a sales target incentive and each has the ambition to be top of the tree. Guess where they will naturally look for the additional business they need? Surprisingly they will almost always hunt on the fringes of their trading territory and often just beyond. Why is this? It's because the grass always really does look greener on the other side of the fence. In short, they will start to compete against each other, not the common rival.

As your organisation grows, you too might find peer rivalry getting in the way of collective success. There are a number of ways to avoid this happening and it is actually good practice to adopt them even from the start. Each makes sense from a logical, as well as a motivational perspective:

- Only reward individual success when everyone has achieved baseline performance targets.
- Make sure that everyone has targets, even the cleaner.
- Involve your team in marketing and training purchase decisions.
- Have both short-term and long-term goals.
- Celebrate success frequently but perhaps in a modest way.

Wordswell – This growing provider of speech and language therapy has a team of front line therapists each working in their local community. To encourage them to actively seek out new client referrals, the company introduced an incentive scheme. Each therapist receives a bonus payment when they bring in a new client. The bonus scheme is linked to their agreed income targets for the firm. It is also capped, so that they cannot exceed what is considered a realistic client workload.

Hygiene factors

It's pretty much common sense that tells us that people are motivated by things like recognition, achievement, responsibility and opportunities for personal growth. American psychologist William Herzberg went further. He looked at the things which can de-motivate if lacking, but will not boost motivation if given in excess.

His theory can be likened to watering a house plant. Give it too little water and it wilts. Give it too much and it doesn't grow any faster, in fact it might even react badly to over-watering. Herzberg saw what he called 'hygiene factors' in the same way. Those he identified included:

➡ Pay – too little is de-motivating, but too much does not give a return on investment.
➡ Supervision – leave people to struggle and they struggle. But over-management also reduces performance.
➡ Working conditions – a negative workplace makes everyone depressed but you can overdo the 'happiness hype' too.

As you build a team it is worth exploring motivation in more detail. You can do this by recruiting a volunteer mentor who has lots of experience of people performance management, or of course you can always buy a book.

In summary

- Organisations need different people at different stages of their evolution.
- All organisations outgrow people; build this into your plans and your culture.
- You need to blend hired staff with freelance and agency people to have the most flexible, cost effective organisation.
- Consider the value of recruitment agencies carefully before dismissing them as too expensive an option.
- Volunteers can add value at every level of your organisation, from top to bottom.
- People are more accepting of goals they have set for themselves.
- Whilst too little pay turns people off, paying too much doesn't make them work proportionately harder.

Find out more

Preen CIC   preencic.org

16

Building Your Community

'We started off trying to set up a small anarchist community, but people wouldn't obey the rules.'
Alan Bennett, *Getting On*, 1972

Building your enterprise family

If you visit rural Africa you will see the power of family. There, people live in small communities of inter-related families where they feel a strong sense of kinship. In the absence of Governmental welfare systems, people support the weak and vulnerable members of their family as a matter of course. It is literally the natural thing to do. Once, it was like that in Europe too, but industrialisation, urbanisation and economic migration have disrupted the natural way of things.

It's one of the reasons we now have social entrepreneurs, to reconnect people with humanity. Few others are as well placed to step back, take an objective view of the landscape before them and work to strengthen people's bonds with each other and with their environment. History is littered with examples of misguided political social engineering. The only people really qualified to make the world a better place are social entrepreneurs; people like you!

Business community

Rural communities in what we perhaps unfairly call 'the developing world' not only have inbuilt, instinctive social care systems. They are also largely economically self-sufficient too. Think back to the history of your own country and you will realise that businesses emerged and evolved to meet almost every local need. The farmer grew wheat, the baker made bread and the thatcher used some of the straw to roof the houses. Barter was as important as cash and everyone knew the importance of protecting the local economic system.

Today, those same business communities interact and support each other as they always have. The difference now of course is that the focus on local, neighbourhood economies has been replaced. We are as likely to buy online from someone 1000 kilometres away as we are to patronise the retailer just down the road.

The impact of this is the loss of the sense of community and mutual support that used to define business communities, particularly in rural areas. Of course, enterprises compete if they provide similar products and services. That is what sparks innovation and the push for competitive advantage.

The Plunkett Foundation focuses on helping rural communities become more self-sufficient. It conducts research and provides practical advice and support to those setting up and running community owned cooperatives and social enterprises.

They were established to:

- seek economic solutions to create social change;
- seek solutions that enrich rural community life;
- see self-help as the most effective way to tackle rural needs.

The Plunkett Foundation helps rural communities re-build their local economies, save threatened rural business and create new ones. As well as providing knowledge and advice, the organisation sets up and manages grants programmes on behalf of funders keen to stimulate rural economic regeneration.

Networking

There are a multitude of business networks. They include Chambers of Commerce breakfast networking clubs, trade associations and professional bodies. Some are national but most are local, providing opportunities for people to meet fellow local business owners.

Networking is a good way for you to build your community of supporters, but you do need to be selective. There are people, for example, who become professional networkers, appearing at every event, perhaps enjoying the social aspects so much that they forget they're there to do business.

Before you attend any networking events:

➡ work out what you want people to do for you;
➡ have your 30-second elevator pitch prepared and rehearsed;
➡ have business cards and make sure your website is not out of date.

 The elevator pitch

This is your standard introduction. It's what you say when you walk up to a stranger in a room and shake their hand. In 30 seconds you need to convey:

• your name;
• your organisation name;
• what you do and who you do it for;
• what it is that you are looking for.

The golden rule of networking is not to try to persuade the person you're talking to become a customer or client. Instead you need to make them an advocate; recommending and introducing you to the people they know. This:

➡ increases your success rate as now you're accessing someone's whole network;

➡ reduces embarrassment as no one likes to be 'sold to' at a networking event.

What works

Develop a networking style that suits your personality and the business you're in. Above all else, don't try so hard you forget to be you!

A social entrepreneur was travelling to London on the train and noticed that the person sitting opposite them was reading an education strategy with which he was familiar. 'I'm going to get a coffee,' he said, 'would you like me to get you one?' he asked.

This broke the ice and when he returned they started to talk. Soon they found themselves talking about the strategy paper they were both familiar with. The entrepreneur found that he was talking to the head teacher of a school in his city. They found they shared many views on the opportunity for schools to become more enterprising.

The entrepreneur followed up the contact later that week and the result was a joint venture, based at the school, providing skills training for adults after school hours. A chance meeting, focused by the social entrepreneur, developed into a successful project.

How to collaborate

Think about a farmer's market. It's successful because the shopper has a wide choice of different produce, from a number of suppliers who share common values. Each sells far more at a farmer's market than they would if they ran a stall anywhere on their own. That's because the market is more appealing to the customer. Where there's more choice, there's also more chance you'll find something you'd like to buy.

In reality, every business can do better by collaborating with others than on its own. The benefit of collaboration extends beyond marketing too. Buying collectively brings down prices. Sharing equipment, people and even premises reduces costs. Plus you have the benefit of a network of people you can talk to. Enterprise in all its forms can be a lonely experience.

Collaborative buying

Almost everything costs less the more you buy. Buying groups are common in agriculture and the public sector. The group collects together everyone's requirements and then invites suppliers to bid for the business.

Even bulk buying copier paper with two neighbours in your office building can save you money. It also saves you the hassle of shopping round for things.

Buying groups offer benefits to their suppliers too. They invoice the group who collect payment from their members by monthly direct debit. The supplier has less paperwork to do and never has to chase overdue debts. Everyone wins.

Here are some very practical things you can do to encourage collaborative buying:

- ➡ Find out what the savings would be from collective buying.
- ➡ Talk to others with similar organisations and suggest shared buying.
- ➡ Consider taking the lead and create a collective buying group.

Anglia Farmers is the UK's largest agricultural buying group with more than 1700 farmer members. It is an Industrial and Provident Society and therefore owned by its members.

Many of the products and services the group buy are things we all use, for example it handles around 7000 mobile phone accounts and buys electricity, gas and private health insurance.

The group also has a growing number of associate members. These are businesses of all kinds, benefiting from the collective buying power of this very large organisation.

It is possible that there is an existing buying group that you could join; you don't have to always start your own.

Collaborative making

Outsourcing has become one of the buzzwords of big business. The theory being the less you do yourself, the more flexibility and opportunity you have. For example, many premium beer brands are produced by contract brewers, with the brand owner also outsourcing distribution and sometimes even sales.

Collaboration is a little different. You might even say more in line with your philosophy as a social entrepreneur. There is sometimes an apparent lack of authenticity with business outsourcing; the brand might suggest one thing and the reality of the product's manufacture another.

Collaboration is more open and transparent. Here are some ways you might consider being collaborative in the way you put together and deliver your products or services:

➤ A group of smallholders create a variety of gift hampers that contain a wide range of the things they grow and prepare.

➡ A Healthy Living Centre provides accommodation to many different therapists so as to create a diverse and interesting customer proposition.

➡ A community café sources its cakes from a mental health project where service users bake on a commercial basis.

Collaborative selling

The farmer's market is a good example of collaborative selling. Together they can attract more customers than they could individually. Another example is Virgin Money, a company that has a very strong brand and positions itself as a champion of the consumer. Many of the financial products it sells are provided by other institutions. Virgin can cross sell products from several providers to their customers.

Just as Virgin can add a marketing skin to the products of other companies, so too can social enterprises be re-skinned by others to become more appealing to the marketplace. For example:

➡ A social enterprise that trains people in catering skills could run a café in a furniture store. The company benefits because they know their customers like to think about their proposed purchase over a cup of tea before committing. It boosts sales. The social enterprise gains because it doesn't have to market its café to attract customers.

➡ A housebuilder offers buyers a gardening service that is delivered by a social enterprise that provides work experience for ex-offenders. The builder gains a point of difference and the enterprise avoids prejudice.

➡ A furniture project, a computer re-seller and an advice agency share premises as they all share the same client group. They create a 'one stop shop' and pool their marketing budgets too.

Collaborative learning

Large organisations have both the budget and headcount required to commission their own internal staff training programmes. Smaller organisations usually buy places on open courses where often the subject matter is almost but not quite what is needed.

Open programmes are always expensive because they cost a lot to market and are notoriously difficult to organise. More often than not, the training provider spends a lot of money on advertising and ends up with fewer paying delegates than were hoped for. As a social entrepreneur, you can help training providers and your peer group by:

→ working out what a group of organisations need and finding a provider able to create a programme that suits your collective needs;
→ persuading large organisations to offer the inevitable spare places they have on their internal training programmes to local social entrepreneurs;
→ building a relationship with your local College or Business School and encouraging them develop and pilot programmes with your people that can be later sold commercially to other social enterprises.

What works

There are often publicly funded training initiatives. Find the people who fund these and form yourselves into a group that matches the initiative's target audience. Then negotiate a training programme that meets both your needs and their output targets.

Finding publicly funded training initiatives

If you look on local Government websites relevant to your part of the world, you will often find strategy documents that outline how skills shortages and gaps are to be addressed. Sometimes they have been translated into tender documents (also published online). When those tenders are awarded, the successful bidder is also named. It is part of the transparency of Government that this information is freely available.

Once you have identified funding and/or organisations focused on your area of sphere of enterprise, you can:

→ pull together a group able to benefit from the training and literally offer the provider or funder an 'outcome on a plate;'
→ discuss how together you might help them make their budget go further by partnering with you;
→ bid for the funding and buy in the trainers you need.

The biggest problem faced by most public skills development initiatives is not delivering the training, it is recruiting the participants.

Online social media and how to use it

Facebook is predicted to grow to more than one billion users, yet it was only established in 2004. The rapid growth and widespread use of Facebook typifies the growth of social media. You probably have a Facebook profile yourself. But how can you use social media as a social entrepreneur? It's one thing to use it to keep in touch with family and friends, another to create and exploit business opportunities.

There are no secrets

Our ancestors had no secrets, because they lived in small rural communities where everyone one was related. Like it or not, social media has created that same level of openness for us all. Google your name and unless you avoid social networking sites, blogs and forums, you will be surprised by what is revealed.

You might not like the idea of people you do business with having ready access to information about your private life. But in a strange sort of way it can be reassuring to be able to glimpse behind the mask of people's business personas. That's not to advocate online stalking; more to say that today, none of us really have any secrets.

The basics

Social media is more about dialogue than selling. Many of the rules of networking apply in a social media situation. In fact it sometimes helps to see social media sites as 'virtual networking events'.

Social media then is about:

- ➡ meeting and getting to know people with whom you have common interests;
- ➡ sharing information, ideas, views and opportunities;
- ➡ building relationships and making introductions, helping those you know, to meet people you feel they will find interesting.

Social media is not a substitute for marketing. It is a deep and fast changing area where it is the users themselves who dictate popularity and lead innovation. Let's take a look at the things you have probably heard of, or indeed used.

Facebook

In a nutshell, Facebook is a website where you can build a public profile, connect and exchange messages with friends, both publicly and privately. You can also chat live with people, add links, share photos and much more.

As a social entrepreneur you will be particularly interested in:

→ providing a window through which people can see that you live your life by the values you espouse in public;
→ sorting and arranging your Facebook contacts so that you can if you wish limit your business contacts' access to very personal content you might want to share with close friends;
→ creating a profile for your organisation, project or campaign that people can 'like' and discuss amongst themselves and with you on that profile;
→ publicising and promoting events, enabling people to be invited and to register all using the Facebook platform.

K-LOVE Radio is a Californian non-profit listener supported Christian radio station which broadcasts in 44 US states and worldwide online. It has a Facebook page with almost 400 000 signed up fans. This means that the radio station can communicate with listeners the world over and more importantly, those listeners can and do give the station feedback and discuss topics with each other. Facebook has enabled K-LOVE Radio to build a vibrant, active online community that hasn't cost a penny.

LinkedIn

The easiest easy way to explain Linked-In is to describe it as a more business focused Facebook. It has much of the same functions and features, but people create profiles that exclusively focus on their career and professional life.

Perhaps the most significant feature of LinkedIn is that people can post recommendations. This enables people looking at your profile to view what others have said about you.

As a social entrepreneur you will be particularly interested in:

→ increasing your profile and helping people find you;
→ the way your profile can boost the Google ranking of your own website;
→ asking questions that experts will answer because doing so raises their own profile on LinkedIn.

What works

Add hyperlinks to your social media profiles on your website and in the footer of your emails. Make it easy for people to find out more about you.

Blogging

Writing a blog gives you the opportunity to share with the world your views on current issues affecting your area of work. They can also form a kind of online diary, where people can see what's new.

You can create a blog easily and at no cost using one of the established blogging websites such as Word Press and BlogSpot. You can also add comments to other people's blogs and join in online debates. Things to remember about blogging include:

➡ search engines like blogs, making them easy to find when someone's exploring a topic;

➡ journalists use blogs to research stories so it's a good place to get 'picked up' if you want to be quoted in the press;

➡ you can embed hyperlinks within your blog so that people can easily click through to your website;

Micro blogging

Twitter is perhaps the best well known micro-blogging site. You can post short blogs, called 'tweets' containing up to 140 characters. Other people can follow your 'tweets' and you can follow others. You might consider using Twitter or other micro-blogging sites to:

➡ share breaking news about your organisation or project;

➡ find and follow like minded people;

➡ ask questions that others might answer within minutes.

What works

Have a social media strategy. Know what you want to achieve, why and how you will measure success. Social media will play an increasing role in business communication and promotion in the future. Be there, but don't let it take over your life.

Your website and how to use it

Every organisation, however small, needs a website. It is increasingly the first place people will go to find out about you and what you do. It is also going to be what creates that vital first impression people form of your organisation, because they will have discovered you whilst searching for something they want.

Creating

When you create a new website you are faced with a vast number of choices:

→ You can build your own site using an online template.
→ You can build your own site using free or purchased software.
→ You can commission a web designer to do it for you.

When deciding which route to take, you need to ask yourself:

→ What do you want your website to do?
  • Promote your outfit and recruit customers and clients?
  • Sell products and services online?
  • Build a community of people?
  • Make documents and files convenient for selected people to download from your website?

Whatever the website is intended to do it needs to be easy to navigate, easy to understand and easy for the visitor to make contact with you when they decide to find out more. You can achieve this by:

→ keeping your basic website very simple and focused, with further pages there for people who want to drill down into a theme;
→ using few words and avoiding those which people will not easily understand;
→ providing case studies and other detailed documents people can download as pdf.

What works

You want to know who is downloading files from your website so that you can ask them how helpful they found it. Set your website so that people have to register with their name and email address before downloading. Then you can follow them up.

Maintaining

By far the easiest way to maintain your website is to use a 'contact management' system. These enable you (and those you delegate to help) to log in to your website as administrators. You can then:

➡ add new content and programme it to 'disappear' when it becomes out of date;
➡ edit your pages and add new ones;
➡ upload documents and images that others can download and use.

The most difficult aspect of maintaining a website is the discipline of setting time aside on a regular basis to do it. Content management systems are themselves usually very intuitive and easy to use. Finding the time to maintain your site is usually harder. Good ways around this include:

➡ making it a regular weekly task; little and often is always better than saving it up for a day when you think you will 'have time';
➡ delegating it to one of your team, or someone outside your organisation who has writing skills and can manage your website for you.

What matters is that your website is always current, fresh and interesting.

Sharing

There are three kinds of documents you might want to share over the internet. These are:

→ advice guides, case studies and brochures that people can download for free;

→ e-books, useful templates and more valuable guides that you want people to pay for (by buying them online using Paypal or similar);

→ internal documents that you only want certain people to be able to access.

Most content management systems will allow you to do the first two. Many include online shopping functionality that you can link to Paypal, your own credit card merchant account or other online payment tool.

Internal documents can also usually be added to your website by creating a secure area where only those who know the password can get in. Many find meeting a barrier they cannot pass annoying and often it's better to share documents amongst your team using Google Documents or one of the many sub-scription sites that provide this service.

 What works

Your website is for your external audience. Internal docu-ments are best stored elsewhere on the web where you can also access them easily.

Search Engine Optimisation (SEO)

Once you have a website you will never be short of offers from companies offering to improve your search engine rankings. That means that when people search for say *'social entrepreneur & leeds'* because they're looking for a potential project partner, if you are a Leeds based social entrepreneur you want your website to come on the first page of their search.

Before worrying about search engine optimisation though, you need to decide what people looking for you might type into their search engine. You might try signing up for Google Adwords which will suggest the most popular words and phrases for your organisation.

Within most content managed websites there are places where you can add these popular search words and phrases. More effective is to use them more than once in the text on your website. That also makes sense because then your website is using the same words that your potential customers use. You can also:

→ comment on blogs because this creates links back to your site;
→ offer articles and content to other sites, in exchange for a link back;
→ have trade links, but only with people you are happy to endorse and who are relevant to your business;
→ caption photos so that they also appear in 'image searches';
→ make sure your website has a site map as search engines use these to reference your website.

What works

Keep SEO in perspective. The better and more specific your website, the easier it will be to find. Invest as much as you can in getting the content right and then do what you can to make it easier for the search engines to bring people to you.

In summary

- The more people you have supporting your venture the more successful you'll be.
- Be selective with your networking; too much can be as limiting as too little.
- Collective buying makes sense and there may well be a local buying group you can join.
- Unusual and interesting combinations of products and services can be very appealing to customers. Collaborative selling can make 2 + 2 = 5!
- Funded training initiatives can often be adapted to meet the needs of the audience if the audience gets together and approaches the provider instead of waiting to be recruited.
- Adding comments to other people's relevant blogs is just as effective as writing your own. Do both.
- Be sensible about how much time you devote to social media. It needs to form part of a business strategy, not be a distraction from business.
- Get a website with a good content management system and make sure you make time to keep it up to date.
- SEO becomes easier if your website contains all the right words before you start.

Find out more

Plunkett Foundation	plunkett.co.uk
Anglia Farmers	angliafarmers.co.uk
K-LOVE Radio	facebook.com/kloveradio

Business networking sites include

• Business Zone	businesszone.co.uk
• Ecademy	ecademy.com
• Network 2012	network2012.net

17

Keeping
Perspective

'All animals, except man, know that the
principal business of life is to enjoy it.'
Samuel Butler, *The Way of All Flesh*, 1903

Work-life balance

There is one aspect of social entrepreneurship that remains to be covered. Social entrepreneurs are almost by definition driven to succeed and so inevitably make personal sacrifices along the way. Passion and a strong sense of social or environmental purpose push you to perform. But you also need to find time to pause, reflect and relax.

Finding time for yourself

Many entrepreneurs will tell you that their work and life are seamlessly linked. They do not differentiate (although their families would probably like them to). However, everyone needs time away from the day to day challenges. Otherwise objectivity and focus slip and you become less effective.

Here are three good reasons to make time for things other than work:

- Just as an engine will rev higher when not in gear and under load, so too will your brain. Even sitting outside with a coffee for half an hour, away from distraction, will help you think more clearly.
- You probably don't have much time to see what's going on in the wider world, outside your work. Go and hear someone speak about a subject unrelated to your own. You'll be surprised how you'll see parallels and perhaps new opportunities.
- Exercise is good for the brain as well as the body. Join a gym, go swimming or even just make time for a brisk walk. If you feel well, you will be able to work harder.

Managing time

You will find it easier to make time for yourself if you are realistic in what you expect to achieve each day. Time management is largely common sense, plus some discipline and a few techniques. Your effectiveness will rise and your stress levels fall if you:

→ make a list of things you have to get done today;
→ set a specific time aside to deal with email, rather than respond immediately to every ping from your Inbox;
→ allow 10% more time for journeys than you expect them to take;
→ keep your workplace tidy and stuff that's not current filed away;
→ schedule tasks, rather than simply work your way through a pile of them.

What works

Always promise just less than you think you can manage. That way if you do more, people will be happy. Over-promise and unless you manage the almost impossible, people will feel let down.

And it goes without saying that you need to make sure you spend time with your partner and family. They should after all, be more important to you than anything else.

Warning: *If you think you can't spare time for your other half, reflect for a moment how much time a divorce would cost you!*

Working from home

Many social entrepreneurs work from home, or indeed wherever they happen to find themselves. Laptop, mobile phone and wireless internet mean that wherever you are, your customers, clients and colleagues can demand your attention. If you work from home, perhaps with a spare room set up as an office, work can intrude even further into your every waking moment.

Yet working at home also has its benefits. You save on commuting time, you save cost and if you have a young family, you can combine work with childcare. Finally, you can work in shorts in the summer and a warm fluffy dressing gown in winter!

If you work from home, you might find it useful to:

➡ have a separate phone line or programme your mobile to use a different ring tone when family and friends are calling. This enables you to filter out the work calls when you're not in work mode;

➡ arrange to hold business meetings in coffee shops rather than invite customers or clients into your home;

➡ have the courage to cut off all business contact from time to time to give you some space. It is after all now possible if you work globally, to have work contacts trying to communicate with you round the clock.

Brightspace opened in 2010 and describes itself as a 'Social Enterprise Park'. It provides offices and workshops, meeting rooms and hot desking to local social entrepreneurs on a pay by the hour basis. For just £50 per month they will also provide a dedicated phone number which is answered for you, voicemail and a range of other virtual office services.

If working at home proves difficult, or you find it lonely, places like Brightspace can give you a base to work from and a ready network of other social entrepreneurs.

A healthy and happy workplace

Managing your own time and stress levels can be difficult. Managing the workload and stress levels of people you employ is a must. It would be counter to your ideals as a social entrepreneur not to care deeply for the welfare of your own people. Yet equally important is to make sure that everyone pulls their weight and does the job they're there to do.

First you need to recognise that employees, however committed to your cause, and entrepreneurs are different.

Employees	Entrepreneurs
Get paid a wage to do a job	Have control of their income, even if they choose to use their profit to do good
Need to know exactly what is expected of them	Have to help employees see how their job contributes to the greater success
May not always have the delegated authority to make the decision	Have ultimate responsibility and accountability

Spotting signs of stress

You have to manage your own stress but when you employ others, you need to keep an eye on their stress levels too. Classic symptoms to notice include:

→ tiredness and difficulty concentrating;
→ irritability and anxiety;
→ over reacting and sometimes irrationally;
→ opting out of the workplace banter;
→ headaches;
→ increasing alcohol or drug consumption.

What works

Every boss gets frustrated but simply dumping your anxiety onto your team doesn't help. It just makes you and them feel worse.

Managing stress

If you are involved in the delivery of front line services, particularly in health and social care, your staff will inevitably be exposed to stressful situations. Dealing with very vulnerable people, or perhaps those approaching death needs lots of sensitivity, compassion and self-control. Providing a release for the resulting tension should be a routine part of your staff care.

Case supervision can go a long way, encouraging front line staff to discuss the emotional impact on them, as well as the practical aspects of the care they are delivering in the field. Sometimes it's a good idea to retain the services of a professional external counsellor, able to help your people finding it really tough.

Stress in the workplace can be very damaging, to people, to profit and to reputation. If yours is a stressful work environment you need to do something about it. To do nothing can cost a lot more.

> **Frank** is a psychotherapist and counsellor. He works for himself and charges enough to provide him with enough to live a modest lifestyle. His motivation is more to make a difference to people's lives than to amass wealth.
>
> He works with a local hospice as well as with a couple of social enterprises that provide care services to the frail elderly. As you might imagine, these organisations have to deal with death on a frequent basis. Frank is retained by the organisations to meet and counsel their staff as and when needed. It helps front line staff to know that Frank is there, even if they do not feel the need to visit him often.

Fun

Work should also be fun. We all spend a lot of time working and may see more of colleagues than we do of friends. Here then to finish are some good ways to make sure everyone has fun at work:

- A graffiti board placed somewhere only staff will go is a great way to let people express themselves in all kinds of imaginative ways. It can also provide a useful barometer of staff morale and provide an early warning of trouble ahead. Always read but never edit.
- Compete against other organisations and teams, perhaps even create a league. It could be five-a-side football or fishing, whatever fits with your people and your sector.
- Create a workplace where people feel comfortable suggesting things that will make work more enjoyable. Be democratic and let everyone contribute ideas.
- Define the boundaries of good taste and propriety beyond which no one should tread. Once you've drawn the line, people will usually respect it.

As a social entrepreneur, you also have the opportunity to keep your people in touch with the impact your organisation has and the work that it does. You will find that as an organisation grows, this becomes harder. You might well have staff working in, say, a shop or driving a van, who have little contact with the people for whose benefit you set the organisation up.

You can keep your staff in touch with your mission by:

- putting case studies on the wall and photos of happy clients;
- giving everyone the opportunity to witness first hand the difference the organisation makes;
- involving them in discussing future opportunities.

Incentives

Performance incentives need not just be about money. In fact you might feel it inappropriate or impossible to incentivise performance. There are also people for whom financial incentives are a turn off; they do the work because they love it.

There is nothing to stop you offering more 'fun' incentives; particularly if they encourage everyone in the team to pull together to achieve common goals. These can be really good fun and highly motivating.

What works

A quarterly staff incentive linked to specific targets works well. Rewards can range from an outing to the seaside accompanied by families, to an evening of beer and bowling. It's not about the cost, but about the way it builds team spirit.

In summary

- Make time for yourself and your family, however demanding your work.
- Manage your time and be realistic in what you set yourself to do each day.
- Working from home can be good, or you might prefer a low cost base.
- Stress can affect everyone. Learn to spot it and deal with it fast.
- Make work fun because that way you will all get more done.
- Keep the passion and purpose of your organisation alive for everyone.

Find out more

Bright Space Social Enterprise Hub   brightspace.org

About the Author

Robert **Ashton** is a social entrepreneur. As well as starting, growing and selling three small businesses he helped set up Norfolk Community Foundation, which in its sixth year gave more than £1m in grants to community groups and social enterprises. He has also started an innovative and successful anti-stigma project and is a Governor of his local Mental Health Trust.

He works with social entrepreneurs in all sectors, particularly health, social care and education where he advises and supports community groups who bid to take over community resources such as hospitals and vital rural services. He is also a challenging and popular conference speaker.

Robert believes that entrepreneurship is an attitude as much as a skill. He says that whilst all successful entrepreneurs take control of their own lives, the best also improve the lives of those around them. They are social entrepreneurs.

Robert would love to hear from you if you think he can help you become more successful. You can contact him at robert@robertashton.co.uk or sign up for his free monthly e-newsletters at www.robertashton.co.uk.

Other Books by Robert Ashton

Brilliant Checklists for Entrepreneurs, Prentice Hall, September 2010

How to Start Your Own Business for Entrepreneurs, Prentice Hall, July 2009

Instant Entrepreneur, Prentice Hall, December 2008

I Know Someone Like That, Turnpike Farm, October 2008

The Entrepreneur's Book of Checklists, Prentice Hall, August 2007

Teach Yourself: Life at 50 for Men, Hodder & Stoughton, January 2007

The Life Plan, Prentice Hall, December 2006

How to Sell, Hamlyn, August 2004

Copywriting in a Week, Hodder & Stoughton, November 2003

Business Alchemy in a Week, Hodder & Stoughton, August 2002

Index